S0-BCI-256

# Eight Minutes
# to
# Better Golf

*How to Improve Your Game
by Finding Your Natural Swing*

By Ji Kim

ST. JOSEPH COUNTY
PUBLIC LIBRARY

NOV -- 2016

SOUTH BEND, INDIANA

Skyhorse Publishing

Copyright © 2016 by Ji Kim

All rights reserved. No part of this book may be reproduced in any manner without the express written consent of the publisher, except in the case of brief excerpts in critical reviews or articles. All inquiries should be addressed to Skyhorse Publishing, 307 West 36th Street, 11th Floor, New York, NY 10018.

Skyhorse Publishing books may be purchased in bulk at special discounts for sales promotion, corporate gifts, fund-raising, or educational purposes. Special editions can also be created to specifications. For details, contact the Special Sales Department, Skyhorse Publishing, 307 West 36th Street, 11th Floor, New York, NY 10018 or info@skyhorsepublishing.com.

Skyhorse® and Skyhorse Publishing® are registered trademarks of Skyhorse Publishing, Inc.®, a Delaware corporation.

Visit our website at www.skyhorsepublishing.com.

10 9 8 7 6 5 4 3 2 1

Library of Congress Cataloging-in-Publication Data is available on file.

Photos by Craig Johnston.


Cover design by Tom Lau
Cover photo credit: Craig Johnston

ISBN: 978-1-51071-1142-6
Ebook ISBN 978-1-5107-1143-3

Printed in China

To my wife, Kimberly

# CONTENTS

# INTRODUCTION

## My Journey

I was born in Pusan, Korea, in 1968. This was during the restoration after the Korean War. At that time, there was little structure in my hometown. It was a time of rebuilding our country. During my childhood, my main focus was athletics. I was very involved in tae kwon do. I started training in it from the age of five and trained very hard every day to become one of the best at tae kwon do. It is what I remember most about my early childhood in Korea. By the age of nine, I had joined the Korean National Team. I remember my last competition was a tournament against the Japanese National Team. It was a lot of fun competing for our country. We could hear chants from our team parents and supporters. I became addicted to competing and winning even at such a young age!

Due to the fact that my parents always worked long hours at my grandfather's manufacturing business, I became very independent. Ultimately, my parents wanted me and my siblings to have all of the opportunities that America had to offer. So, the day I turned ten years old, my mom, sister, and I moved to America, on December 10, 1978. We landed in Palm Beach, Florida, before driving to Stuart, Florida, our new hometown, where we lived for almost fifteen years.

After coming to America, it was like a rebirth, starting over in a completely foreign land. I remember desperately seeking consistency in my new life. I did not speak one word of English. I had no idea what anyone was saying for months. I attended Parker Elementary School in Stuart. My experience in an American classroom came as a big shock. Children were talking in the classroom and doing things that never would have been allowed in my classroom back in Korea. The language barrier was such a challenge for me. Since I didn't know what anyone was saying, I thought they were making fun of me, even though that was probably not the case.

But I soon began to acclimate to my new environment, thanks in large part to my teacher, Mrs. Brado, who was my first English teacher and who took a special interest in me. She took her teaching profession beyond the classroom for me because I was the only foreign student at the school, and she treated me like I was one of her own children. The first time I ever had fried chicken was at her house. Boy, did I love Kool-Aid, fried chicken, and mashed potatoes. I was in heaven! One night I ate so much of it I got sick all over their table.

The Brados would have me speak English when I was at their house. I would tell them stories about the fishing adventures that I had with their son "Bert" while we were on summer break. Mrs. Brado was very instrumental in teaching me to speak English without an accent. I am forever grateful that she cared to go the extra mile for me so that I was able to learn to speak English so well.

In my life, Mrs. Brado is the one person I will never forget. In a small way, I try to repay her by taking an interest in my golf students the way that she took an interest in me. I hope one day I can make a difference in someone's life the way that she made a difference in mine.

I guess you are wondering how a kid from Korea, new to America, wound up taking up golf at such a young age. Well, it all started with my sister, Kim, who was at Martin County High School at the time. Her math teacher asked her to join the ladies' golf team. The PGA of America gave her her first set of golf clubs. When she came home with that bag full of clubs, I was intrigued. I followed her to the driving range the next day, and the rest is history.

Even though golf was not very popular at the time, I had found a sport that I could again train for day and night! I practiced all day on the weekends. Since I lived in Florida, I could practice every day after school all year round. I truly loved the game and still do. Golf gave me a great deal of satisfaction, and it became my new passion.

In the ninth grade, I met Clark Collins. We both loved golf. We played all the time. His father was a lifetime PGA professional. At the time, he was one of the best teachers in the Metropolitan New York section. One night, he saw me practicing on the range. He came over and told me that if I could practice the way that he was going to show me, I would be a high school state champion one day. He was right! In 1987, our varsity golf team at Martin County High School became state champions. This led the way for me to chase my dream to play professional golf. I wanted nothing more than to play on the PGA Tour.

During my teenage years, I had many great friends (some my age and some quite a bit older) who loved golf. One of them was a man named George Cisar. He was from Chicago but spent his winters in Stuart. When I was about fifteen years old, Don Padgett, who is a past PGA president, introduced me to George, who was probably in his early seventies at the time. When he was young, he was the Chicago amateur champion. His influence in golf in the Chicago area is legendary. I never knew this until after he passed in 1993.

George taught me so many wonderful things about the golf swing. One day, I was struggling with my ball striking. He gave me a tip in a song. He was whispering and singing, "You hold with this, you hit with that!" I wasn't shifting with my hips. I was using my hands too much. He was trying to help me remember to get my hips into the shot before I made contact. Remembering to do this made a great difference.

George used to say that my golf swing reminded him of Arnold Palmer's. He also commented that I was more of a hitter of the ball than a swinger of the club (as someone like Jack Nicklaus was). I remember many conversations with him over cups of hot chocolate in the mornings before playing golf together. He taught me many things about life and the golf swing.

After high school, I turned pro. I was so fortunate to have the opportunity to pursue my dream as a player on the PGA Tour. But after three years on the mini tour, I decided to take a break from the tour. I took my first teaching job at Precision Golf in San Antonio, Texas, under the direction of Jim Barker. This is where I found my true calling in life as a golf instructor.

I have had the great fortune to work under some of the top teaching professionals in the business, including Jim McLean, Craig Harmon, and Hank Haney, just to mention a few. It is my greatest passion to share with you my philosophy and instructional methods to help you achieve the level of playing that you desire.

## My Philosophy

From learning the game myself and from teaching thousands of students for almost two decades, I came to the realization that there are so many different things that influence the golf swing. But there is one part of the basic technique that influences the swing way more than any other. It has been the focus of my teaching for almost two decades. It answers the question of why we see so many golfers with such diverse movements in the golf swing. What I have found with astounding consistency is that the hitting zone determines the outcome of the swing. The hitting zone principle is simple, but most instructors seriously neglect it.

The mystery is not due to lack of knowledge, but rather the simplicity of this technique. I have heard so many different reasons why golfers seem to be struggling with their swing. Most golfers believe the trouble stems from their head position or their hips on the downswing. It has been interesting to see the severity of this position cause so many problems in their swings. When this technical position is not found, the golfer will have many years of bad golf without much enjoyment. The zone will not be easy to master, but it is a must for all golfers who want to improve their game and get the maximum enjoyment out of playing golf for many years. Once the correct diagnosis has been issued, the golfer can see an immediate improvement.

So many golfers take lessons for many years and are never able to take their game to the level that they would like. Golf is most difficult when players reach the level where they are trying to shoot lower in the 70s or even into the 60s. The game then takes on a different dimension. The mental aspect of the game comes into play. At this point, the golfer must be competent at all of the fundamentals of the swing to score low. It is very challenging for a golfer to go from scoring 75 down to 72. It can take years to achieve this. Those two or three shots are so hard to shave off. It is much easier to reduce your score by 10 or even 20 shots or to go from shooting in the 100s to the 90s. The game can be made easier when the focus is right and the golfer is practicing with a purpose. There must be a focus on what to practice on the range. Practicing incorrectly can be avoided.

It is most important to remember that each golfer has one swing when hitting the ball. You will change the dynamics of the swing depending on which club you are using. As you move through my book, you will see illustrations of each part of the swing along with a detailed explanation of how to hit each club.

At the beginning of any great golf swing, you must have a pre-shot routine that helps you focus. Every great player starts his or her pre-shot routine the same way for every shot. Focus is very important in playing great golf. You must be disciplined at focusing on one shot at a time, giving every shot the same care.

The grip is what gets your swing started in the right direction. There are illustrations in this book of the three types of grips that are used. It is important to choose the grip that is most comfortable for you.

Before you grab that club out of your bag, it is important to evaluate what kind of shot you will be hitting. You need to ask yourself a few questions. First, how far is the ball from the hole? Is there any wind? And is the shot uphill or downhill?

I believe that everyone has a natural swing, and it's important to nurture that swing and improve upon it. Rebuilding a swing is so very difficult and may not end up being the correct swing for you. For example, Tiger Woods is still searching for his swing, and in the process, he has lost his natural swing. Playing with your natural swing is very important. Your natural swing is a swing for life. There is no right or wrong swing. It is a matter of what swing gives you the results you are trying to achieve.

*Note: The instructions in this book can be emulated by right-handed golfers. Left-handed golfers, in many cases, will have to complete the exercises in a way that is the opposite of the manner directed.*

# Section I

How to Be Brilliant at the Basics

# GRIP NATURALLY

## Grip Position

In terms of grip, preference is not a fundamental, but comfort is a must.

The **Vardon grip** is referenced as an overlapping grip. It is most commonly taught by the American and the European teachers. The pinkie overlaps the forefinger of the glove hand.

**Vardon grip**

Jack Nicklaus and Tiger Woods most notably use the **Interlocking grip**. Although it is not the most commonly used grip, the grip does have in its favor the fact that two of the best players of all time have championed its use. Here, the pinkie interlocks with the forefinger of the glove hand.

**Interlocking grip**

The **Ten-finger grip** is the most natural grip for beginners. Ed Fiori was the first person to beat Tiger Woods in his prime with this grip. This grip is best for players with smaller hands. It promotes a lot of hand action. Sometimes called the "baseball" grip, it is formed by holding the club with one hand on top of the other.

**Ten-finger grip**

It doesn't matter if you hold the club with a Vardon/overlapping grip, an Interlocking grip, or a Ten-finger grip. What matters most is that you are comfortable with your choice.

Jim Furyk, a multiple PGA Tour winner and one of the toughest competitors on tour, overlaps two fingers over the grip hand. No matter how you hold the club, the function of the hands depends on the pressure points of the hands. If you put the correct pressure point on the grip, then the grip comes together almost perfectly, giving it functionality. In the following pages, I will show you some ways to bring the magic of proper gripping together while gripping the club your own way. This will give your grip the functionality of a tour player. Pay close attention to the two pressure points that will help you to have a great grip for the rest of your golfing life.

## Grip Pressure

The pressure points in the grip are as important as the correct position of the grip. To get the grip into your ideal position, hold the club up above the ground with the clubhead approximately at eye level. Place both hands on the club comfortably. After you have placed both palms on the club, the key here is to wring or squeeze both hands in the opposite direction as if you were wringing a towel. With both hands in a wringing position, the left hand should be on top of the grip as the right hand palm is overlapping the left hand and the grip.

Using the sternum as a reference, notice the "v" formed by your forefinger and thumb on your left hand. When the "v" points to the right shoulder, this is known as a strong grip position.

Comfortably bring the club together with your hands. As seen here, the grip shows a lot of gap between the glove thumb and the rest of the glove hand. The entire thumb is shown here.

Pretend the grip is a wet towel, and with both hands wring the towel to get the water out. This allows the hands to work together and puts pressure more in the fingers of the grip, where it should be. Notice that the thumb and top of the glove disappear while showing the knuckles of the glove hand.

If your forefinger and thumb point to the left side of the body, this is known as a weak grip. A strong grip tends to close down the clubface at impact and will make the ball pull or hook. The weak grip tends to open the clubface, which makes the ball push or slice. I have seen balls slice with the strong grip and balls hook with a weak grip. It is all in the way the hands work to position the clubface in the swing.

It is without a doubt that the focus should be on keeping control over the clubface. Where your hand position is on the club is most important. The "wringing the towel" drill correctly positions the club in your fingers, and from there it allows the club to move freely. Almost all amateur golfers prefer a strong grip position.

When your grip is too strong, the ball will not get into the air high enough and will make the golfer hold the release throughout the swing. This also causes the hanging back and chicken-winging of the arms. However, the weak grip creates the opposite problems. It often causes the golfer to hit the ball too high and to cast or release the club too early. This will cause the golfer to hit behind the ball and create an all-arms swing.

When you do it properly, the wringing motion will put pressure on the bottom of the last three fingers on the left hand. The top of the hands, especially the forefinger and the thumb on the right hand, will feel pronounced. When you do this, you will begin to feel the arms now connecting to the body. This is the third connection in golf. This is not stressed enough. The best players in the world emphasize how the arm connection is so important in hitting consistent shots.

The wringing motion with the hands will now position the arms where they should be as you are now getting into the correct setup position. This tension you feel in the upper arms and in the chest is the correct feel. The arms are now balancing on the body, and the body supports this position where the arms can be in a soft and relaxed position. From this point, you will find the arms are in the optimal position.

Next, I am going to discuss a great way to organize your grip with your stance. Stand straight up, and then bend at the waist. This is approximately a 30-degree bend from the waist. Let the arms fall and drop toward the ground with the club in your hands. This is your address position. Your biceps will feel tension in the connection, while the elbows will be in a locked position holding the arms in the correct position. Doing this at setup will create a simple position where you will have the arms and the body in the correct angle so that the body can move in an athletic motion. Once the arms, elbows, wrists, and other parts of your body are in a locked position, you will need speed and good athletic motion for a good swing. This position feels more like a linebacker getting ready to defend an opponent than a golf stance.

The key here is the grip position and grip pressure. The correct grip pressure will place the grip in the proper position on the club. It is best to make a routine of placing your hands the same way on the club every time. Then you will place your hands by feel and not by just a correct position. I will say this about the grip—it has to feel correct each and every time, and what each shot requires is that you feel your hands on the club. Too often, we are told where to hold the club without an explanation of why we are doing it. If you are holding the club with the wringing motion on the club, you will find the correct position of your grip. This allows you to line up correctly for the swing. This keeps the arms in the proper position at address and during the swing.

When new golfers set up this way, they are surprised when their punch shots feel so good. But they often don't realize what they did correctly to get that good shot. What has happened is that they are using the correct arm and grip positions. This is the same sensation/motion that you would feel in your arms if you were chopping wood. When you are swinging the club, you will feel the body leveraging the swing when arms are in the correct position. You will not see the arms hanging away from the body; rather, the arms are pulling toward the body at the finish. This is why the best swings are so well connected, with the arms and body working together.

When trying to get the right feel before a shot, a lot of pros keep gripping their club. When they are doing this, it is the wringing position that they are working on. This helps them to feel the hands and arms better. The pressure points of the grip do not change during the different stages of your swing. When you start your backswing, the left hand feels more pressure on the back of the hand where the last three fingers of the grip are. It is more of a pushback with the hands. The club will also feel heavier on the bottom end of your left hand.

During your swing, your body should be in motion with your hands. Your hands at the beginning will feel as though they are working slightly under and up. Your hands should not rotate immediately; rather, they should move in a one-piece motion. At the beginning of the swing, the body is holding its setup position. Your hands and arms in the first stage of the swing feel reversed in the rotation; rather than to the right, they move left. It will not look that way, but this is the correct feel to get the first move right.

The next position allows the club to set at the halfway point in the backswing. In this position, you will feel more of the right hand, wrist, and arm pushing the right elbow into the body as both hands are fully cocked. The pressure should be on the lifeline of the right hand at this moment as the thumb and forefinger flex. At the top of the backswing, the left hand and wrist should balance the club underneath the thumb. The thumb should not be on the side of the grip, but directly on the bottom of the club. This helps the golfer make a smooth transition from the top of his or her backswing to the initial downswing.

## Making the Connections

The squeeze position from the upper arms and body ensures they are connected and working together in the correct sequence.

The "wringing the towel" drill will connect the hands on the club and position the arms correctly.

The pressure points in the photo on page 11 are located in the hands and in the arms at the setup, which then form a perfect triangle in the center of the body. This gives the club a center point where the bottom of the arc is presented in the swing. This pressure point is crucial in maintaining the proper connection in your swing. Without this connection, the rest of the swing will be in a corrective mode. The touring professionals are always feeling this in their swing. They get this position organized before they swing the club.

As the feet are to the ground, the club is to the hands. There are two connections to the grip. The other connection that is most important is the one between your arms and your body. When you have connection in the swing from the beginning,

you will make solid contact. This is due to the fact that solid contact does not occur consistently without the body and arms working together—especially pre-impact, impact, and post-impact. The feeling of staying connected is in essence the most important one a golfer can experience in his or her swing. That is why there are so many drills that the professionals work on in their daily practice sessions and before tournaments.

What is a connected swing? The feeling of being connected is to have both upper arms staying tight against the body. The upper arms and the chest are coming together. The pressure is nice and snug at this point in the address. The sensation of wringing the towel will give you that feel. It is by far the simplest illustration to give you the feeling of the chain reaction of the hands to the club and arms to the body. Jack Nicklaus has always talked about creating the triangle in his swing to promote "togetherness," which was the key to his swing. Watching films of Jack showed me this position. When I show my students this position, they progress much faster. This is the key setup position.

A great grip equals a great player! I grew up hearing this from my teachers. They always referred to all the champion players of the past who, like Sam Snead, advocated for holding the club in a certain way. They were right! It worked for them, and it was/is the correct grip for them, as they have won many tournaments with it.

After watching many tournaments, I noticed that the players with so-called nontraditional grips and swings were winning. This is also true with tour players. Back in the 1980s, when Lee Trevino and Bill Rogers were playing on tour, they both had nontraditional grips and odd-looking swings. They won many tournaments, and each became the number-one player in the world.

For a long time as a kid growing up playing and observing the game, I was critical of someone who did not have the same grip as the one I used. I assumed he or she did not learn correctly and would suffer on the course. After I started competing, one thing became crystal clear: the kids who had the poorest grips could win tournaments. This was the first time it hit me that the grip was not a fundamental.

The grip is just the beginning of the story. You will find the right grip for you. You'll know you've found the right grip when you can hit straight shots.

# ADDRESS THE BALL WITH A PURPOSE

## CHAPTER 2

## Playing inside Your Feet

Golf is played on the inside of the feet. Top players are brilliant at it. You must pinch both knees inward inside both feet to ensure that you turn against the inside of the right knee on the backswing for solid contact. A good drill is to place a beach ball between both knees at address and hold it while completing the backswing.

The inside of the shoulder line should be directly above the knees and the balls of the feet, as shown here. The rear end should be on the outside of the heels for a good balanced setup.

This allows the weight to be centered over the feet. Both legs and arms must be parallel at the setup position.

The center of the body should be just slightly behind the ball. The right shoulder line is positioned inside the right foot. This will allow for a nice pivot point, keeping the weight on the inside of the right foot on the backswing. Swaying outside that right foot will cause random contact with the ball, causing you to hit behind the ball. The left shoulder line is positioned above the left foot, so as you move through the ball, it can allow for the weight to shift forward toward the finish. This produces good footwork, creating consistency and solid contact. Without this position, it will be hard to coil on the backswing and release fully toward the target. Notice that the back foot is square and the front foot is open, ensuring that on the backswing you build resistance while on the forward swing the body can fully release toward the target.

## Athletic Setup

One of the first steps in starting the swing is to kick-start it. Being stagnant causes tension.

At the setup, your body maintains a calm and focused position. From there, you will need movements that will allow your swing to have a flow that will create rhythm and a tension-free swing. The best players in the world from the inception of the game all have this characteristic. From Bobby Jones to Jack Nicklaus, they both had their own way of doing this. Bobby Jones did this with the movement of his right knee and hands. Jack Nicklaus did it with combination of his head movement, setting it to the right, plus the kicking of the right knee. It is a preference of each golfer to do this his or her own way, but to do it is a must in order to start a good rhythmic swing and a good fluid takeaway.

Notice the right knee from above the setup to the start of the swing shown here. The right knee has kicked forward, and the hands are slightly forward. This is the beginning of the movement into the backswing. Without these slight movements forward, there would be too much tension in the hands, which would kill the swing.

During the first part of the takeaway, the right knee goes back to where it started from, as the pressure points of the right knee are holding the lower body to build resistance and to eliminate any sway away from the ball. Next, the shoulders are pivoting, as the left shoulder is now level with the right shoulder, and the arms are in the same triangular position from the start. This allows the club to stay low to the ground as it starts back. Moe Norman, a world-renowned ball striker, set his club and started from this position, a foot away from the ball. He said he never got this part of the swing wrong!

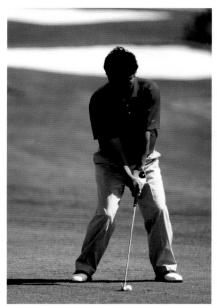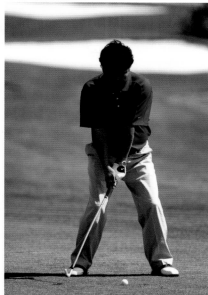

At the address position, a waggle can be an important part of keeping the body loose and the mind focused on the target. There are many forms of waggle or movement in the golf setup as you address the ball and prepare for the shot. Many players do so with the waggle of the golf club with their hands and arms as they look at the target and then glance back at the ball. There some other players who waggle with their feet and body, such as Mark Calcavecchia, the former British Open Champion who is now on the Champions Tour. His waggle is unusual, because he waggles his body as he moves his heels and feet by jostling them as he looks to the target. He does this instead of moving the club.

Jason Dufner waggles the golf club with his hands, swinging them back and through, in a manner more pronounced than any other player on the PGA Tour. He waggles them three or four times before he goes to his backswing. I've learned a lot

from watching players' waggles since I was fourteen years old growing up in Martin County, just north of Palm Beach. I used to watch Gary Player and Lee Trevino waggle when I was a kid. I liked the way they took their waggle, where they steadied themselves at address. They both stared at the target. They had a lot of movement before their swing, especially from the hands and feet. It was a continual movement before their swing.

Every chance I got to watch them practice their pre-shot routine, I would practice what they were doing. I tried to implement what they were doing into my routine, because it fit my personality and the pace was comfortable for my swing. It doesn't matter what waggle or pre-shot movements you make during your address position. The key is to focus on what makes you feel tuned in before you begin to take your backswing. From the beginning, as you are standing behind the ball visualizing the target, you prepare to lock in on your shot. Next, try staring at your target and then glancing back at the ball.

Remember that at address it is important to have physical movements that allow you to absorb the shot you're trying to hit. That feeling just can't be described, because it is so personal. Whether you're hitting a short shot or a long shot, once you have determined how you're going to hit the shot, your body can start to engage in all of the necessary preparation.

There are so many different ways that the greatest players have addressed the golf ball. Their movements have been unique in the way they prepared to begin their golf swing. Bobby Jones, who was a winner of the Grand Slam back in the '20s, was one of the greatest golfers of his time and had a very graceful waggle and smooth setup. He had a setup that was very repetitious, with different movements for all of his shots. When I was growing up in Stuart, Florida, I got to watch Jack Nicklaus when he was practicing at Frenchman's Creek with his teacher, Jack Grout. I always noticed the intensity and the way he stood over the golf ball at his setup. He hit his shot with a more deliberate and tighter stance, engaging his arm muscles at the address. He looked as though his swing was about to explode just before taking the club back, and I didn't notice a fluidity about him that would fit my style. He was great at how he did it, and if it fits your style to stay over the ball like Jack did, then mimic his moves at your setup. He's not a bad one to copy. After all, he did win eighteen major championships.

# Section II

Finding the Natural Swing

# FOCUS ON THE BACKSWING 3

## The Right Way to Start

Notice the right knee from above the setup to the start of the swing, as shown here. The right knee has kicked forward, and the hands are slightly forward, to begin their movement backward. Without these slight movements forward, too much tension is created in the hands, which kills the swing.

Errors come in multiples of two; you make one error on the backswing, and another error will be made to compensate. Be careful how many errors you make on the backswing.

The shoulder pivots, as the right side is now higher than the left side. When the head is still, the pressure goes to the left knee and the inside of the right hip, creating the correct pivot point in the lower body. The arms create the correct width away from the ball. The right arm stays on top of the left arm. This space between the forearms stays the same as it was in the setup. The pressure point is now on the left arm's biceps, near the chest. Many pros hold a glove or a towel under the left armpit to feel this connection. At this point, the right hand is in a "shake hand" position.

This is a good checkpoint to ensure that the club is starting on plane. The shaft at this position disappears, and the head of the club is rising above the right forearm. The toe of the club is pointing upward toward the sky.

On the next page is a close-up of the hands and the club at this position. Notice that the leading edge of the club is perpendicular to the ground and is above the right hand. There is a slight gap between the forearms, ensuring the arms are starting to rotate. The shaft disappears at this position, and the hands are in line with the target.

Loading up to a powerful position will ensure the correct movement on the downswing for a solid contact. Being on a correct swing plane will help you with direction and narrow your dispersion rate.

The upper body is behind the ball, while the lower body is holding down the resistance. The right knee and hip are angled like a tripod; they are in the same position at address, with the right hip turned against the inside of the right foot. Imagine the right leg being positioned like that of a pitcher on a mound. The weight is loaded up on the inside of the right leg while you turn your upper body again to the target. This creates a powerful backswing. You are now ready for the downswing. In this position, the body is two-thirds on the right side and one-third on the left. The key pressure point is on the inside of the right foot and knee. The left arm and club are in an "L" position while both elbows are parallel to the ground.

At address, the club sits approximately at a 45-degree angle. This angle should be the reference point during the entire swing.

The address position presents the swing plane, or the angle the club should be traveling throughout the swing. There are fourteen different clubs and fourteen different swing planes. But it is important to use the same swing to achieve this.

When you move into the backswing, as illustrated at the top of page 27, it is necessary to load up to a powerful position that will ensure the correct movement on the downswing for solid contact. Being on the correct swing plane will help you with direction and will narrow your dispersion rate.

At the halfway point in the backswing, the shaft of the club is above the original shaft angle. The size of this gap is as important as the angle it sits on. The shaft angle should bisect your right shoulder. Refer to the photo at the bottom of page 27.

There is a slight pause at the top of the swing. This is where the change of direction is important to create leverage and the dropping of the shaft. Look at the photos on page 28, at how the shaft gets closer to the right shoulder. The shaft narrows, and the weight starts to shift toward the target. From this point,

as the weight reverses toward the forward swing, the arms will start to close the gap, as you will see on the downswing. The shaft needs to travel down toward the ball, maintaining the

same angle. This allows the club to come from the inside of the ball.

## Stay Connected

Byron Nelson referred to this position as one of the most important positions of the swing. He felt that if you made an error in your swing in the takeaway, especially from the first three feet away, your chances of making a good shot were slim. We now know errors come in twos. If you make one on the backswing, you make another one to compensate for it on the forward swing.

Golfers make a lot of errors by thinking in multiples. This is why I fix so many interesting swings that have a lot of movement. The golfer is compensating during the swing, trying to correct each error, thus creating a great deal of movement. I would emphasize that there is no perfect swing. There are only more efficient swings and more repeatable swings.

It is important to focus on taking the club back correctly. Ask yourself what that position is and what it feels like. It is best to practice the backswing by taking the club back to about three feet away from the ball. Feel the lower body hold the position. The pressure is on the inside of the right leg, and now at this position, the left knee is pulling forward. The pressure builds slightly toward the left knee. The hands and arms are pushing slightly away from the body; as you go into the backswing, it begins to lift the hands, arms, and the club (see previous photo).

If you are looking down on the club at this point, the head of the club has not rotated yet. The club is in the same position as it was at address. The hands and forearms also look as if they have not had any rotation to the right yet. That will be the next step, the body starting to rotate and naturally allowing the forearms and hands to rotate back.

Next, the right hip and shoulder start to rotate back as the arms are getting ready to set the club in balance.

This is where the body continues to rotate and coil firmly against the right side of the swing. As the body rotates to create a full coil, the arms, hands, and club lift up so that the arms are above the right shoulder on the backswing.

The pressure of the right hip builds greatly on the backswing. Like that of a discus thrower, the lower body has the same coil. Its job is to create power from the ground up. To do this, the feet need to initiate the coil from the upper body, using the ground as leverage. By the time the hands and arms are to the halfway point of the backswing, the body is coiled almost 80 percent full. The body does this to create stability, while the arms control the club. The club is now pointing straight up in the air, and the body has made a nice coil back. The left side should feel slightly lower than it did at the address position, as the club has not yet turned over to the full backswing.

Now, the weight distributes itself in multiple places during the swing. The reason we are trying to perfect all of the positions of the backswing is for the "moment of truth" (as we call it when you are making contact with the ball). You will need to time the right sequence of the swing; otherwise, you will have a good swing that hits mediocre shots.

Most golfers have the motions of the swing correct. But what's lacking is how that motion is utilized and the timing of it all. That is the essence of what my teaching is all about. It's about helping every golfer utilize his or her natural swing.

What is your most natural swing? Your natural swing is a swing about which you don't have to worry that it's going to look the same way every time. It is the swing that is more effective when pressure is on it during a match. You will get the natural feeling of your swing once you have practiced enough.

When your swing is at the top of the backswing with the momentum ready to change direction, there is a slight pause at the top. The weight then begins to shift forward. Now the hips rotate fully on the backswing, the right hip locks in on the buttock, and you will feel lots of pressure that builds up on that end of your hip and thigh. That is a good thing, since it tells you your lower body has fully rotated at the top of the swing. The arms should feel very high in the air. That momentum allows the arms to swing away from the body. The arms are creating a lever so that they can swing down with speed to catch up to the body. That means that the arms do one thing while the body has other functions during the swing.

During the backswing, the body is rotating and shifting the weight back. The important thing to remember with the body is that it mainly turns on the backswing with a slight weight shift. Then there is a lateral move that shifts the weight forward, which allows the weight to shift completely.

Another way to accomplish this is to practice on the range, pulling your left arm up while holding your left wrist. Put the right hand on the wrist of your left hand. From the address position, pull up and support the left arm with the right hand. Move your left arm as high as it can go, up and above the right shoulder, while keeping the left arm straight.

This will help you to keep the arms moving up during the swing with very little tension. The right arm helps support this backswing drill. At the top of the swing, the right arm should feel a lot of pressure holding the left arm up. You will now swing through to the finish. This allows the club and hands to be held high throughout the swing and its shaft plane to create a position where the arms have freedom to swing and for the club to come in and out of the necessary swing planes or its angles.

This drill is to correct the arms that are being pulled inside on the backswing. Once the arms are pulled inside, they will be stuck there for the remainder of the backswing. The club then will have this over-the-top motion that can hit a weak slice or a hard pull, depending on how you end up after you make corrections for your errors during the swing. The right foot should be firmly planted at the time, and there should be no swaying at the top of the backswing. The back foot is similar to that of a pitcher on the mound, in that the weight is positioned on the inside of that foot and is in a ready position so that you can push off that foot when you are prepared to make the forward transition.

There are many ways to achieve an effective backswing. These are the more important things to consider while working on your backswing. Simply put, the arms go up and the body rotates. When you put these two together, you are creating the maximum power in your backswing.

At the top of the swing, you can that see the entire back is facing the target. This illustration shows the chin touching the shoulder. The left arm is relatively straight as it creates back-swing width, which represents a powerful position.

Halfway on the downswing, the shaft and left arm form an "L" position. The body is now beginning to cover the ball. From here, most golfers will look similar.

The right knee is feeling a lot of pressure to push the weight forward and transfer it to the left leg. As the right foot pushes

forward and up, the left knee is taking on the pressure of the transfer of the weight. The left thigh and knee start to build resistance. Then the weight transfer takes place. The key here is the sequence of motion that allows the upper body to remain coiled while the weight shifts forward. Some of the best players, such as Ben Hogan, thought this was the most pivotal moment to create massive strength and energy in the swing.

This is the halfway point in the downswing; the shaft angle is closing the gap toward the original shaft angle set at address. This means that the arms at this point are halfway down toward impact. The club is in balance and is seeking the hitting zone. The club still maintains a parallel position of the swing angle or the target. The left arm at this point starts to rotate inward closer to the body. This is where the connection between the left arm and the body begins. Many golfers who fail to rotate the left arm inward to reconnect the arms in this lowering position tend to get the club underneath the swing plane. When the club gets stuck under the swing plane, it creates havoc for low-handicap golfers who fight the hook and push in their shots.

Harvey Penick, author of the *Little Red Book*, referred to this position as the "magic move." From this point in the swing, it will determine if you are going to hit the shot successfully toward your target.

The club is parallel to the ground and is pointing toward the target. The shoulders and the center of the body and knees and hips are facing square to the ball at this point. Get this position correct, and you will be hitting many fine shots that go directly to the target. The wrists are still in a fully hinged position, which means that the club still has not been released during the swing. The hips are pushing as the butt end of the club is pointing at the target and the pad of your left hand is leading the way toward the ball.

The hands are in the delivery position and are just above the right thigh. The right knee is on the inside of the feet as it moves toward the ball. The wrist is still fully hinged, and the right elbow is moving along with the right side. The arms are connected to the right side as it moves toward impact.

The right ankle has rolled toward the inside of the foot as the weight starts to go from heel to toe, pushing up from the foot. This creates the forward movement. The shaft at this point has disappeared and sits on top of the hands, which are underneath the chin and in front of the toe line.

The moment of truth! The left wrist is flat at this position, while the hands are in front of the clubhead.

The feeling at this point is that the left arm begins to gain tighter connection as the left hip and torso are rotating toward the target. The right arm is also beginning to straighten out or extend. The right side is now starting to cover the inside of the left shoulder.

You are now at the impact position of your swing! The body is in rotation at this point. The left hip, left arm, left shoulder, and left knee should be turning tightly around the left side. This allows the right side to release and deliver power. The club is automatically squaring up to the target. The left side of the leg and hips are starting to appear from this view. The right side is

releasing, keeping the body's balance, while the right shoulder stays level through the shot. It is important to see the right arm on top of the left at impact.

## Power Moves

Creating a powerful coil on the backswing is as important as trying to create a powerful downswing. This puts you in a position where you can uncoil your body on the downswing. It is necessary to identify the backswing power moves and to know how to put them together. This is so that they can become one continuous full motion, allowing the transition of the downswing to reach its most powerful position.

First, you must take the club back in one piece. From your setup, your arms and shoulders create a triangle between them. From there, the club should be pointing directly at the center of your stomach or slightly toward the left side. The club will need to go back to about three feet away from the ball. You must maintain that same connection to where the butt end of the golf club still aims right at your stomach. What you are doing is creating enough width in your backswing that creates the coil. Remember to take out the small-muscle move, which means snatching the club back with your hands and picking the club up with your arms. This way, you're keeping the hands and arms passive as you are creating a huge coil with your upper body, while keeping your knees flexed and leveraging against the right leg and inside thigh muscle. At the address position, the club should be directly in front of you, with both the right and left arms straight, so the triangle is maintained. At address, remember to have a wide base, which will help you to leverage your lower body and create more power in your swing. Remember that all of these powerful positions on the backswing are designed to initiate and engage the downswing transition by using the most powerful position to create power on the downswing. I remember watching Ian Woosnam, who is only five foot four. He hit the ball longer than anyone on the PGA tour. Observing his backswing, I noticed that he took the club back with a big arc and in one piece, using his big muscles in his swing. It was then that I realized it wasn't the height that created a big-arc golf swing, but it was rather the utilization of the big muscles that created tremendous power in the swing. I then started to try and mimic that move on my backswing. During the summer of my high school senior year, I became one of the longer hitters on my team. This strong one-piece takeaway on the backswing is a great move to maximize power in your swing.

The second power move is when your arms are about shoulder height, and your shoulder has turned nearly 90 degrees away from the ball. Your wrist needs to be fully hinged at this position. This position loads up your hands and arms so that the wrist can snap at the bottom of the club with a lot of force. This position must be formed in order for you to bring the club down efficiently into a delivery position where this power source can be utilized. Having a strong hip position can add tremendous power to your golf swing. It also creates the right sequence on the downswing to where it allows the release of your swing to happen at the right time. At this point, the right hip has turned nearly 45 degrees away from the ball, and pressure is starting to build on the inside of the right leg, which is acting as a power position for the downswing.

The arms must create leverage at the top of your swing for power. Once you have completed the coil and have fully hinged your wrist, the next power move is to push the arms up as high as they can go while bringing the club's shaft parallel to the ground at the top of the backswing.

It is important to remember when you are starting your backswing to take the club straight back, keep your eye on the ball, and keep your head steady, looking down. These are all good tips, and they are appropriate for all golfers. But having all of these thoughts at one time can have a disastrous effect on your swing. The game needs to be made simple. So how do you do that?

One way is to go through the swing one step at a time. Set up steps to guide you through your swing to establish a pre-shot routine. Swinging the club should be a natural fit with hand-eye coordination. That part happens in a flash of a second. The first time I ever saw myself hitting a ball was when a tournament volunteer took a picture of me during a golf tournament. I was shocked to see that my eyes were closed at impact. Obviously, I worked to keep my eyes open at all times during my swing.

The things you can control about your swing are the basic fundamentals. Once you have accomplished this, your natural instincts and movements will happen automatically. Learning to be brilliant at the basics are some of the lifelong lessons of many golf professionals. It seems that no matter how many years you play golf, the fundamentals remind you to keep it simple and not overthink the swing.

Addressing the ball properly is very important. When you are setting up, you should first take a shoulder-width stance and stand straight, with your hands to the side. Push your hips back and allow your spine to lean forward while keeping the lower back straight. That should put the angle about 30 degrees between the hip and spine. Flex your knees slightly and feel as if you are sitting on the edge of a seat.

Be sure that your body is balanced over the middle of your feet. Avoid leaning forward toward your toes or backward toward your heels. This position is similar to that of a downhill skier who is coming down the hill. It is an athletic position that allows you to have the correct balance and leg power at the beginning of your swing. It is important to let the arms hang straight down, soft and relaxed. Clasp your hands together and grip the club. This is a basic setup position.

The next step is to find the correct ball position. The ball is in the center of the stance at this point. Your ball position is very important. The ball position can be different for each shot. Ball placement is what makes all shots unique. When you are hitting a driver off the tee, the club must hit the ball on an

upswing or ascending angle. This means that the ball needs to be placed toward the front of your stance. You must be tilting toward your back foot so that when you follow through from your backswing, you will have the trajectory you are looking for from your driver.

In most cases, it helps to use the natural loft of the club to get the ball into the air. Playing the ball in the front of your stance will also help to get the ball into the air. When you are using the 3, 4, and 5 irons, you are hitting the ground, but the divot should be a thin strip. The only clubs with which you will begin to feel a large, deep divot will be your wedges or your 9 iron. If you are taking large divots with your lower-lofted clubs, it means that the swing is coming down on too steep of an angle to the ground rather than being level with the ground.

If you are taking too deep of a divot when you are using the high-lofted clubs, you are digging with the edge of the club. This can be avoided by not overswinging with these shorter clubs with loft. In a normal 5 iron setup, the ball position is slightly in front of your sternum. The ball should be placed underneath the left side of your chest. The weight balance being 50 percent–50 percent with this club, the club should be swung approximately 80 percent of the full effort. With any club with higher loft than a 5 iron, the 80 percent rule is in effect for control.

It is important to swing in balance. That is why the setup is about the "sit in" position as you begin the swing. As you sit in, the feet and knees need to feel the pinch between them, especially the right knee. The weight has to be on the inside of your feet. This will hold you in place better, and you will more likely avoid swaying during the swing. Any time the weight gets outside your feet, the body will tend to drift. Also, whenever the weight gets on the outside of your feet, it will cause too much movement in either direction, resulting in random missed shots.

# FOCUS ON THE DOWNSWING

## CHAPTER 4

## Athletic Sequence of Motion

The athletic body motion sequence, which includes good mechanics, is essential for an effective swing. Yes, the backswing is very important, but remember you do not hit the ball on the backswing. The downswing has its own sequence of motion. Shift, rotate, and then hit. When you do this effectively, you will make solid and consistent contact during all golf shots.

The images on the next page depict a drill you can do to get the feel for the movement that will allow you to create proper and athletic movements. The head movement is exaggerated in all three illustrations. Incorporating these movements will help the muscle memory: 1) the head is behind the ball, 2) while the head stays on top of the ball, drive the body forward to a point where the right knee is on top of the ball and 70 percent of the body is in front of the ball line, 3) the only thing left on the right side of the swing is the ankle.

The only time you would not use this drill is for specialty shots such as a flop shot or in a greenside bunker. When you make these movements in the correct sequence, you will create what I call the flat left wrist at impact. These moves create leverage and power that you can control when you are hitting the ball solidly. Hitting shots with consistent distance means you are making solid contact in the middle of the club. When you are mishitting the ball on the random parts of the club, you will vary the distance too much and you will not be able to control the distance of the shot.

To illustrate this part of the swing, imagine you are in a rope-pulling contest. You pull the rope with all of your body leaning and leveraging. All of the weight pushes from your feet, grabbing earth and using your lower body as you are pulling against it with your upper body. This is the way you get the most from your weight and strength. This is the same move you make when you are shifting your weight on the downswing. Even though you do not have a rope to pull, you must create an action on the downswing that gives you resistance to swing around. You leverage against the left side with your legs. You are doing this in the swing with your lower body. The feet, knees, and hips create this resistance against the upper body.

During the downswing, the feet should push the entire body forward. The upper body and the lower body will have a lateral shift. The key to this move is to use your feet to push the body forward, instead of holding the weight back, which will cause you to cast the club toward the ball. This move shifts the weight while you are fully coiled on the backswing. Then the next move of rotating happens. If it is in the proper sequence, the body creates this move to leverage the body while the arms and club are at the top of the swing, creating a slingshot effect.

I have noticed that the more separation a golfer can create at this position, the more powerful the golfer's swing will be. This takes some work outside the golf course and in the gym. Getting your body in good physical condition will improve your golf swing. The better shape your body is in, the better your swing will perform.

The left arm and the club are now at a position where they are forming an "L." They have now moved from being all the way at the top of the swing to where the arms have dropped to your upper sides.

The right arm is very tight against its side, as the angle in the right hand is very tight. This tension in the hand and wrist is good. It is necessary to feel the tension at this point, confirming that you are creating power in this sequence.

The lower part of your body should be pushing hard from the right foot. Now the arms should lower into the delivery position. The hips are pushing forward, and so are the right hip, knee, and leg from the right foot. The right knee should also be working inward toward the ball and closing the gap while getting closer to the left knee. This helps you to begin firing the right side. I encourage all of my students to practice doing these moves without a ball to acquire muscle memory.

The feeling here is that of a punch shot, as if you were in the trees making a recovery shot. What you are trying to create is the feeling of the arms pulling in toward the body and hitting against it as you feel the rotation of the body and arms. Then the hit comes. That hit should feel as though the club is thumping the ground. Rotation can create incredible amounts of power. At the beginning of the swing, the right wrist is set in a hinged position. The wrist will remain in the hinged position during the backswing and downswing. The right wrist feels tension and is in a tightly hinged position the entire time until after impact (see photo on page 45).

Finally, on the downswing, the sequence of how the body moves is very important. The sequence of Shift, Rotate, then Hit, is the correct sequence of your downswing. Using this sequence will create power and efficiency in your swing.

## Start with the Hips, Then the Legs

First, the hips are pushing away from the original top of the swing position, and the knee is closing the gap. This ensures that the weight is on the inside of the feet and staying stable. It is almost as though the left side has hit a wall, and now it's the right side's turn to come to the ball. This happens only when the body rotates into the ball. As the body rotates into the swing, the visual you want to have is the butt end of the club pulling toward the target (see photo on the top of page 46).

This allows the club to create a gap between both elbows. The left arm creates more separation, as the right arm is tucked into the body even more. This is where the power starts to open up in the swing. The left arm at this position creates separation, while the right arm is tight up against the body and the club is lagging. This is the beginning or first part of the rotation, as shown at the bottom of page 46 and top of 47.

The next move in your downswing is to rotate the arms into the body as the body starts to rotate inward toward your left heel. The left hip at this point is pulling the hardest toward the target. The arms are closing the gap between them and the body as they work toward the impact position. The key move here is to reconnect the arms from a delivery position to an impact position. The club is pointing down at the target line and is parallel to the ground at your hip level, while the hips are pulling the arms in toward the pocket of the left hip socket, near the thigh area.

This can be a good practice position. Take the backswing to the top, and feel the downswing to the impact position in one smooth stroke. When you hit and stop, you will feel the body holding its resistance. This should give you the feeling of a punch shot, as if you were in the trees making a recovery shot. What you are trying to create is the feeling of the arms pulling in toward the body and hitting against it as you feel the rotation of the body and arms pulling through the shot.

Then the hit comes. That hit should feel as though the club is thumping the ground. Rotation can create incredible amounts of power. Remember, the wrist is set at the beginning of the swing. The right wrist feels tension and is in a tight hinge position the entire time until after impact.

Because of how fast the release is during the swing, the only thing you feel is the re-hinging of the wrist after impact during the follow-through. It is only after impact that you should feel the release.

Until then, your right wrist is hinged, especially just before impact, when the right wrist pushes from the lifeline of the right hand in toward the left palm. The left hand should be in a flat position, where the knuckles feel almost like they are in an exaggerated position pointing downward. This is the supinated position for your left hand (see first photo on page 50). The left hand is formed from a good hold from the right hand. A bowing action is needed with the left hand. This position is one of the fundamentals that are not discussed much during the swing, but it is what most professionals do during the swing. Most high handicap amateurs are in the opposite position when it comes to the wrist position and club position at impact. Most of the time, their left wrists cup, causing an open clubface.

This position is created properly only when you follow the correct sequence in your swing. If you are flipping your hands at impact, you are scooping the ball into the air. This will hurt your performance, because it will not be aligned with the physical motion of the swing. What happens is that you will do all you can to help lift the ball up into the air. The wrist position will be in a scoop position, where the left wrist cups instead of being in a flat left wrist position.

When the ball is on the ground, you must hit down. That thought is counterintuitive for a beginning golfer. The following will solidify how the club should be at impact—the right hand should feel a slight hinge in the wrists and a slight pushing feeling from the lifeline of the right hand. Now, we are at the impact zone. The push from the right hand is a necessary thrust to release the club at the proper moment during impact. The club reaches its maximum speed just slightly past the impact zone. When this happens, the club is swinging in the right path or motion.

When we review video of the high handicappers' swings, we see that they are in the opposite position at this stage of the swing. What we see is that their weight is on the back foot at impact, which pulls the arms up, creating what is commonly known as the chicken wing (see image below). When this happens, your arms will be in a pulling motion toward the body instead of swinging toward your target with your arms extended. The other outcome is that you will either hit ground first (a "chunk") or you will top the ball (a "skull").

To correct this, shift 70 percent of the weight onto your front (left) foot and have the right knee pointing toward the ball. Your head should feel like it is over the ball and not behind it. Your right shoulder is also on top of the ball. This allows the hands to stay ahead of the clubface.

Here are a few things to consider regarding how the ball gets up in the air properly. The golf ball is designed with dimples on it. These dimples allow the ball to rise in the air and stay up in

the air while spinning. The way the club gets the ball into the air is by creating a descending blow to the ball using the ground as the friction. The amount of angle in the shaft indicates how high you are sending the ball into the air.

Hitting the ball with high velocity does create more spin. So if you are not hitting the ball very high with the right technique, it is due to the lack of speed. To help with that, do not change your swing; rather, get a club that has more loft to start the ball higher. There are new hybrid clubs that will make the ball fly with less spin and bore through the air, giving you more distance and control. Playing with fitted clubs will help you achieve this. It makes playing the game easier. Knowing more about the equipment you are using will help you improve your swing. Selecting the right shaft flex, loft, and length of the club is an important part of having the right tools at hand.

Understanding what the proper impact position looks like will help you to improve making solid contact. The most common fault position occurs when the weight shift is reversed, with the weight on the back foot and the arms pulling up to scoop the ball at impact. This also comes mostly from an incorrect perception of how the mechanics of the swing work to get the ball up in the air. The most common thought about the impact position that ruins many golfers' swings is the notion that you must scoop the ball up in the air. You must do the opposite! You must hit down on the ball and shift the weight on top of the ball, toward the target.

Staying in the correct impact position is key to hitting great shots. It might feel odd, as it may be a position you have never felt before in your swing. Comfort is the enemy of improving your swing! This is a good thing to remember. When you are getting the true feeling of the correct swing, you will achieve the consistency that you are striving for. Understanding this concept will enable you to enjoy the game as you work toward your dream round of golf.

As the club approaches the delivery position, which is right before the impact position, the sides of the arms are away from the body, and the club is above the original swing plane. The arms and the club will now work inside the body (see below).

The downward motion is what creates leverage in the arms and brings the body to the ball with full force. The left arm is working hard to clear the body to get out of the way to bring the right side through. At this stage, the arms are in a fully extended position so that the only thing that is lagging behind is the clubhead. At this point, the club still has not made contact and has not flexed the shaft forward yet. It is still stored energy until impact.

As we discussed, there is a negative chain reaction if your weight is back on the right foot, with the left arm bending, the left shoulder lifting, the left wrist cupping, and the arms pulling up toward the body. Take each component of the swing if you are in these positions, and reverse these movements.

Above are the "chicken-wing arms," which pull inward toward the body.

## Arm Extension with a Release

To do this, push the weight forward to where it's 70 percent on the front foot and 30 percent on the back foot. Allow the arms to straighten while turning the body slightly toward the target. Keep both arms straight, as shown on page 55. Then hinge the wrists so that the club is lagging behind. Be sure at this point that the butt end of the club is past the ball while holding the lag in your wrists. This is a very good thing to happen at your impact zone, practically reversing all of your bad swing habits.

The drill that I use most often to show my students where the club is bottoming out at the right place and at the right time is the "line drill." This drill is a very effective tool that will give you instant feedback after the swing. Many professional golfers use it to master consistency in their swings. If you are not doing this drill correctly, it will tell you immediately. You can do it on the range or on the course.

To practice the line drill, you will need to draw a straight line from your ball to your stance. Stand over the line, and make sure it bisects the middle of your feet, as shown on page 56. Practice making divots past the line to ensure you are making solid contact with the ball.

With a 5 iron, your goal is to make a swing and see where your club bottoms out in the swing. If it hits anywhere on the line or before the line during your practice swing, this drill will show you that you are not shifting your weight properly. The body may also be late in getting to the ball during the follow-through.

If you are struggling to hit past the line with your full swing, stop! Break this down into smaller swings. First, practice hitting past the line with a small swing, like a pitch swing, but be sure your weight is leaning forward and the club is passing the line in the middle of your body. The club should be bottoming out

approximately six to eight inches past the line. This ensures that the club is always making contact first. Next, hitting the ground past the ball means that the lowest part of the club is hitting the ground, which is happening past the ball. This move is very important in all shots. This is one of the more important parts of the swing, since it is about impact and making contact.

This next drill will give you instant feedback. I call this the "Focus Line Drill." Focus on swinging the club and hitting the ball then the divot afterward, which is past the line, as shown at the top of page 57, in these divots.

Finally, on the downswing, the sequence of how the body moves is very important. This sequence of Shift, Rotate, then Hit should be the correct sequence of your downswing. This will create power and efficiency in your swing.

## How You Should Look at Impact

At the impact position, there are a couple of things that are crucial in order to achieve the effectiveness of good contact each and every time. Being consistent at this position will be a big factor in becoming a good player. There are so many ways that the golf swing can move from the beginning of the backswing and into the downswing, but the most common theme evident in every great golfer who plays the game is that his or her impact position has the same dynamics.

The shoulders, arms, and wrists and down to the shaft should form one straight line. This straight line is different from that of the golfer who enters the impact position with the left wrist cupped or broken down at impact and with the arms and elbows bent. When amateurs look down the shaft of the club, the clubface has passed the hands at the impact position. This is what I see so many golfers struggling with. Golfers must understand the importance of the proper impact position happening in their swing in order to take their golf game to the next level. When this happens, they will have a consistent swing.

Although impact is a result of the first transition from the top of the swing and all of the chain reactions that occur leading into the impact position, understanding the correct position will help golfers to appreciate the differences between how they are coming into the ball and the proper way to be in a solid impact position. Working backward from impact to the backswing can help you to change the mechanics of your downswing.

Casting the golf club and coming over the swing plane are two problems caused by an incorrect downswing transition. Your weight shift and feeling the proper impact position will help you make the transitional change on your downswing. Because that movement is an athletic movement that is used in other sports, you can transfer that feel to your golf swing. An example of this is when a hockey player makes contact with the puck. He first has to shift his weight onto his front foot, then rotate his body, and finally swing the stick at the puck. That is the sequence of a powerful and athletic motion.

To feel the rotation that allows the club to make consistent contact with the ball, you should transfer your weight onto your forward foot while pulling your hips to the left. This rotation from your hips allows your torso to encourage the straight left arm and shaft to form a straight line. The harder you pull from the hips, the harder you will begin to feel the top of the left wrist pulling up, and the more likely that a bowing shape will occur on the wrist.

This allows the club to stay down and through the ball, helping you to compress the clubface onto the ball longer and producing solidity in the shot. When it hits that sweet spot of the golf club, there's no other feeling in golf that feels as good. At this point, the right wrist has a pinched or a slightly cocked feel. In this position there's a significant increase in the size of the crease of your wrist and hand. The palm of your right hand should feel as though it is pointing down toward the ground. As the club releases past impact, the right wrist will straighten out. At the moment of impact, it should feel like a considerable amount of angle has formed between the right wrist and the right forearm. That is the opposite of flipping the wrist, which is what a lot of amateurs do at impact. If you don't feel this in your right wrist during your swing, you must practice this move without a golf ball until you have mastered it.

To do this, make small swings from the address position and bend the right wrist back without breaking it and move forward to impact, allowing the left wrist to lead the clubface and letting the right wrist maintain that angle. You will feel your hands pull your weight forward and clear the hip out of the way so the hands, arms, and shoulders can form a straight line in front of the golf ball. Be sure that the alignment of your shoulders and your forearms are parallel to your target. While this happens, your hips should be at least 15 to 25 degrees open to the target as you feel the weight pushing down onto your left foot. The weight should be more on the heel of the front foot, allowing the proper hip rotation to take you into the proper impact. When you look down, you should be able to see the back end of the shaft, because your head remains behind the ball, and when you look down at the clubface, you should see it de-lofting. Now the leading edge is flush with the ground.

A good practice drill to do is to address the ball as you would with a 7 iron or a 5 iron, making sure that your weight is evenly distributed and taking the club back halfway up to your waist. Once you feel comfortable doing this, you can add the golf ball to the exercise. Begin by hitting some mid-iron shots, striking them lightly. You should still be able to feel the club compressing into the ball and the ground. Hit the shots no more than 50 yards in distance. The ball will fly low to the ground more than usual and the ideal is not to lift the ball up in the air but to drive it low and thrust your body and club into the ball. As you start to become more comfortable with this drill, do it with a longer swing, increasing the length of both the backswing and the forward swing. Do this until you can swing halfway back and halfway through to get the feeling that the momentum of your swing is moving into the proper impact position. Striking these shots may produce a feeling that you may never have experienced before.

This move is also important in driving the golf ball and in pitching. No matter what you are trying to accomplish, since the ball position is different for driving and for pitching, you will sense a slight difference in the dynamics. This is because in driving you are hitting the ball on the upswing because the ball position is toward the front of your stance and the ball is on a tee. No matter what club you choose, you are using the same technique in coming down to the impact position. This will help you to experience, perhaps for the first time, the feelings that come from hitting a golf shot properly.

Many golfers who have played the game for many years have never truly felt a solid impact and the solid contact that is produced with this correct fundamental technique. Once you have mastered this skill you will want to repeat this position over and over again. Knowing where you need to be during the swing and where you need to be at impact will greatly increase your chances of improving your swing.

# FOCUS ON THE FOLLOW-THROUGH

## CHAPTER 6

## The Post-Impact Position

The first stage of the post-impact position occurs when the club is starting to reach the fastest point in the swing. The left hip and left shoulder have cleared out of the way for the body to begin to pivot off the front foot. At this point, both arms should be straight and the right knee and right heel are beginning to work inward toward the target.

This is where the clubhead reaches its maximum speed during the swing. When practicing swings for this position, listen for the sound of the club. Be sure to listen for the loud swooshing sound on your left side during your practice sessions. This ensures a powerful release.

From this view, the toe of the club starts to point toward the target, as shown in the first image on page 67. The right arm is beginning to release over the left hand. The shoulder and hips are beginning to open up toward the target. At this point, your chest and hips are seeking the target. This position is the reason why so many great golfers such as Annika Sorenstam and David Duval look slightly untraditional. Their head moves toward the target along with their hips and chest. This movement is very important to continue swinging toward a good finish. This is one of the reasons why they are such great ball strikers.

Halfway through the finish, the arms form a triangle in front of the body. The body has control at this position. The arms are moving in connection with the body. Get this position right, and you will swing in the correct sequence. The mechanics will

keep your shots very forgiving. You will notice that the right hand has crossed over the glove hand (see second image above). This happens naturally when the body rotates properly.

The butt end of the club is in line with the center of the body, the chest, and the stomach (see top of page 68). At this point, the club is working together with the body and achieving the correct sequence.

Notice the parallel target line and the body line position in the photo in the middle of page 68. The club is on the target line for a split second, just at impact. Then, the club must swing left along with the body so that it moves away from the original ball line but is parallel at this point. The hands and arms begin to disappear from view. The arms must swing around in the same direction because the body's main job is to turn. The chest and sternum must be turned toward the target to get a good turn on the ball for power and consistency.

On page 69, you'll see the reverse "L" position on the follow-through. In order to ensure the proper finish, you must do

three things correctly. First, exert light grip pressure so the club flings past the hands with lots of speed. Second, your shoulders must pivot correctly so that the right shoulder has passed the

left shoulder from the 90-degree angle and is now closer to the target. Third, your chest and sternum are in a direct line to the target. The right heel should feel light, and almost all of your weight should be transferred onto the left side at this point. Next, the weight on the left foot is being placed on the outside of the heel, and the inside of the left foot starts to lift slightly. It is important to note that when your body is rotating hard through to the finish, this is the natural tendency in a proper finish. All great players rotate to the outside of the front heel. Many high-handicappers tend not to get into this position, since they are not rotating to the finish.

The next photo provides a better look at this reverse "L" position. It is an important visual for the proper release point from this position. The head starts to rotate toward the target. The chin is now touching the right shoulder, as the shoulder is now the key to finishing the swing. The chest should be facing the target at this point, as the body and weight move toward the target. Three-quarters of the weight exchange has happened,

and the turn has been completed. The right arm has dominance over the swing.

The left hip is working hard to get out of the way for the proper release. The club then finds the swing plane. A better swing with solid fundamentals, such as a good grip, can really help keep the clubface angle square.

It's important to note that the right shoulder on the follow-through brings the chin and head up near the finish. The eyes are still slightly tilted, and the right side is chasing the target. The right shoulder is past the left shoulder and beyond the 90-degree point. The hips are now reaching the 90-degree point. The upper body is coiling on top of the left leg as the right knee comes closer to the right thigh.

Some professionals drive hard from the lower body, and as a result, the right knee actually touches the left thigh. This is a good exercise for someone who comes over the top, which happens when the upper body dominates the first part of the swing. Working the feet, knees, and hips first allows the proper weight transfer for solid contact.

Looking from this view, the hip and thigh line are one piece. If you can see your left hip pocket, then you are not following

through properly and will lack consistency in distance and direction.

The club shaft returns to the approximate angle where the shaft originally began. The key here is to release the club back to its proper swing angles. The club, arms, hands, and body all need to rotate to the left side and clear for the right side to work toward the target line. The key to a powerful and accurate swing after impact is to allow the left arm to fold and the right arm to extend while the right side, including the right shoulder, works closer to the target.

Maintaining a good body angle to the finish is a must in completing the swing. The spine angle should be in the same position as it was at address, and at this point the right arm is fully extended while helping the left elbow rotate and fold down to allow the right shoulder to keep working toward the target. Allowing the right shoulder to work toward the target is one of the most important ways to bring power and full efficiency to the swing. The right side must chase the target for consistent swings and ball direction.

A well-balanced finish is a result of good rhythm and tempo!

Holding your finish to evaluate the shot is a must. You need to ask yourself if the ball went the way you expected it to. If

not, what went wrong, and can you identify the errors? This will help you with your next shot. The body has now aligned with the left leg and is in a tall position with all the weight transferred to the front leg.

At the finish, the shaft lies across the back of the head, while all the weight has transferred to the front foot. As you can see, the right heel is completely off the ground and on top of the toes at almost 90 degrees. From this view, you can see the complete backside. You can also see that the upper body has coiled more than the hips. Whereas the hips rotate at a maximum of 90 degrees, the shoulder turns between 100 and 120 degrees. This is especially true for professionals like Tiger Woods and Michelle Wie, whose swings show an exaggerated rotation at the finish. This is due to how hard they swing. The harder the swing that is accompanied by the proper technique, the more rotation it has. It is created by momentum in the post-impact position. As I have mentioned countless times in this book, the second part of the swing is where the club travels the fastest. For most high-handicappers, we notice that the fastest part of their swing is prior to impact. This causes casting in the swing, which leads to inconsistent contact. It also affects power.

Gaining control of every swing enables you to control the finish. This allows you to swing in rhythm and utilize no more than 80 percent of your full power during the swing. It helps to make better contact with more consistency. Striking the center of the clubface also helps to control distance. This is what the pros do. High-handicappers are swinging 100 percent each swing. This hurts accuracy and direction. It is necessary to find your 80 percent swing.

## Hit It Dead Straight with the Four Straight Lines

There are many aspects to hitting the ball straight as an arrow. The most imperative is that the club travel down the target line, with the clubface pointing straight at your target. There are many different ways to take the club away on the backswing. Again, the whole objective is to deliver the club three feet from the ball to three feet past the ball, traveling down its target line parallel with the clubface square at the target.

There are four checkpoints during the swing that help you to be more consistent with this move. At setup, you must square up your shoulders; forearms and club face the target. At impact, it's important to assume this position to allow the flow of the arms, hands, and the club toward the target. Your feet and hips do not have to be in a parallel position, as many great ball strikers address the ball with their hips, knees, and feet both opened and closed. It doesn't matter what your preference is. The hips must be slightly open at impact to allow the body to rotate through the ball to create power and consistent contact during the swing.

### Four straight line positions:

During the swing, there are some important positions that create the four straight lines in the golf swing. In the photos on the next two pages, notice the two straight lines on the backswing and two straight lines on the forward swing.

On the backswing, the club should be parallel to the ground and pointing at your target line. The club is parallel to the target at the

top of your swing. The club should point at your target on the down-swing at the same place where it was parallel on the backswing.

The last parallel position of the club is post-impact. When the club is level with the ground at this point, the club points directly at your target. Let's discuss how to accomplish these positions in your swing so that you can learn to hit the ball dead straight. These are what I call the four straight lines to accomplish consistency in the golf swing.

By making slow-motion swings that stop and go and by making checkpoints, you can succeed in hitting the ball in a straight line, without even needing to hit a golf ball. This is a drill that helps you to put the club in these positions for four sequential moves.

From the setup, place a club parallel to your target line and lay it on the ground. This can be a great source of information, working as your guide in checking these positions during your swing.

First, be sure to stop and check when the club is parallel to the ground that it is pointing at your target line. The toe of the club is now pointing up to the sky at 90 degrees from the ground.

Second, at the very top of the backswing, be sure the club is parallel to the target and the toe of the club is hanging down to the ground. This ensures that the club path and the clubface are both square to the target on the backswing.

Third, on the downswing, bring the club to the delivery position. This is where the shaft points parallel to the target and the toe of the club is pointing up to the sky. The point to remember at this position is that your right arm is tucked up against your right side, where it is folded, and the right wrist has maintained a fully hinged position. Your left wrist is now flat, in a straight line with its forearm. Your chest and shoulders now should be facing the ball and your shoulder at this position should also be parallel to the target. The hip at this position should be slightly open, as it is beginning to rotate into the forward swing.

This delivery position is the moment of truth, and from here no changes can be made except to continue through the ball. The outcome will only be a result of how you have delivered the club at this position.

However, you can get this wrong if you don't achieve the follow-through correctly. That is your fourth position in this process.

This fourth and final position is reached by rotating the hips and the body through the ball where your chest is now covering the ball going past impact. At this point, both arms, especially the right one, are beginning to straighten out and extend. The club now reaches the maximum clubhead speed.

When David Duval and Annika Sorenstam were both the number-one players on the PGA tour and on the LPGA tour, respectively, they released their eyes and even their heads toward their targets. At this post-impact position, this move allowed a very nice flow without any interruption in the follow-through. This is important for any golfer who struggles to hit the ball consistently. The randomness comes from the body stopping at impact, thus quitting on the ball.

This only happens when you are thinking about keeping your head down and your body down during the golf swing. I mention this because this is one of the thoughts that most amateurs are thinking about when they're hitting the ball. I hear it over and over again from amateurs when I ask what they are thinking about during their golf swing. When a player is thinking this, too often he or she quits rotating through the ball. It is very rare to hear a tour player making a comment about keeping his or her head down, eye on the ball, and not lifting his or her body. This is not what pros think about. It's the opposite. They are thinking about trying to get through the ball.

The fourth parallel position is where the club is level to the ground and where the shaft points directly parallel to the target. The toe of the club is pointing to the sky, mimicking the first parallel position on the backswing. The body has now rotated to where the chest and the belt buckle and even the head have rotated, working toward the target.

I can't express how important this forward move is in order to make clean contact with a fluid follow-through, so that you are avoiding a stuck position on the follow-through. This is also the main reason why golfers create a chicken wing in their swing, which is the bending of both arms at the post-impact position. Without the full extension at the post-impact position, it is not possible to accelerate through the finish.

# Section III

Driving Fundamentals

# PLACEMENT

Driving the golf ball is most often thought of as how far you can hit the ball off the tee. But that can't be any further from the truth when it comes to playing your best golf. The best drivers have always been the players who can drive the ball in the fairway and in the right place for the next shot. It is all about placing the golf ball on the course for your approach shot, which is more important than distance. Ben Hogan, one of the best drivers of the golf ball, often said, "It's never about how far you can hit it but where you hit it that matters the most." I believe that this is something that you should always remember when you are driving the ball. There are many players who hit the ball long, but the ball ends up being in the trees or in the rough. Being out of the fairway or in the rough puts them at a disadvantage, even though they drove the ball farther. It is best to hit more fairways and place your drive where there is optimal position for your next shot to the green.

Sometimes your driver may not be the best club off the tee. Just because you're on the tee box doesn't mean that you must use your driver and try to hit the ball as far as possible. It is better to hit a 3 wood off the tee, which will enable you to place the ball at the right spot on the fairway. This is especially true if the driver will put the ball in a bad spot for your next shot. If you have a tendency to slice the ball or you have a problem with the direction of your driver, using the 3 wood would definitely allow the ball to go straighter. This is because the 3 wood creates backspin. The driver will spin the ball sideways more than any other club.

If you have problems driving the ball with a slice, a 3 wood could be the answer for hitting the fairways more often. If you hit the 3 wood off the tee, you will not lose as much distance as you might think. You may lose only 20 to 25 yards in distance, but you will catch more fairways. It is worth the sacrifice. You will find that you can make more pars and birdies from the fairway picking an extra club or two than hitting balls off the fairway or out of bounds in the trees. Those are not good options when you want to keep your score down.

There are some players who will hit their driver every time, and that may be the best part of their game. You have to be disciplined enough to strategize your game if you want to lower your score. It is wise to remember that more pars and birdies are made from the short grass than from the rough or the trees!

As the saying goes, there are a lot of long hitters in the woods! Getting fitted for your driver using the latest golf equipment technology can really help with controlling a slice or a hook. Keep in mind that the position of your ball for the next shot is more important than how long you hit the ball. Be sure to pick the right club for positioning the ball in the best spot for your next shot. Remember, it's only the beginning of the hole. Usually, there are other facets of the hole after you drive that will challenge you. So do not get yourself into trouble immediately off of the tee. Learn to hit more fairways by understanding the best way for you to be the best driver off the tee.

# THE GROUND IS YOUR ENEMY CHAPTER 8

The ground is your enemy! Avoid hitting the ground when driving.

The driver swing is the same as the iron swing, but it has entirely different dynamics and fundamentals. Knowing these important differences will help you become a better driver of the ball.

Remember to sweep up! Do not hit down on the ground with the driver. Letting the club hover above the ground helps to keep the body standing tall. This allows for a good driver swing. Hunching over is bad for a driver swing. Some of the best golfers in the world and legends such as Jack Nicklaus, Greg Norman, and Tiger Woods all use this simple method for great driving.

They set up tall, and the last thing they do is lift the club and let it hover above the ground and then swing.

The two vertical lines represent an ideal balanced setup. The butt line is outside the heel. The shoulder line is in line with the knees and the toe line to help counterbalance the weight. Favoring too much weight forward toward your toes where your

shoulders are over the toe line encourages an over-the-top move during the swing and falling forward during the finish. Putting too much weight back or sitting back too much toward your heel encourages a flat backswing, which will put you in a corrective mode throughout the swing. At the setup, arms should be soft while holding the club with light pressure on the grip. Remember, the driver is the lightest club in your bag and also the longest. It achieves the greatest impact from tension during the swing. Keeping the hands and forearms soft and having thoughts of good rhythm and tempo are musts for good driving.

Pictured below and on the next page are face-on views and target line views in three beginning sequences. The first position from the front view shows the upper body beginning to load and turn on the back leg as it builds resistance in the lower body

and creates upper body rotation. Shoulders are starting to get behind the ball. From the target-line view, as you are looking directly at the target, the club shaft is absolutely parallel to the target. The only thing you see here is the clubhead in line with your swing plane. The second photo shows that the club is set with the shoulders and upper torso nearly 80 percent coiled. The arms and club are in an "L" position, while the arm is level to the ground; but notice that the body is nearly in a fully loaded position. This is a swing that is more controlled when pressure is on it. With more pressure, this type of backswing allows the golfer to let go of control and perform the swing, allowing the results to take care of themselves. The final position is the full backswing. Notice the shaft is above the head, creating a wide arc. In 1999, Tiger Woods did this the best and was rewarded with accurate iron drives.

The driver swing plane is the flattest swing plane out of all fourteen clubs in the bag. The shaft is on plane with the target. The body at this point is pulling the hands down, reacting to the change of direction. The wrist is fully hinged, as the hands are halfway down while the club is still pointing up in the air.

The on-plane swing in most cases contains the angle in which the club needs to travel to master consistent golf shots. The wrists are fully hinged as the right forearm points to the ground. The right arm is now connected to the right side, and pressure starts to build on the outside of the arm. Pushing down on the right elbow pulls the shoulder down and raises the left shoulder. The feeling on the right side is tight up against the body at this point.

This is where the release happens in the arms during the swing. The arms should create speed through here to get the release to square up. Make sure your chest is facing the ball as you are bringing your arms down. It is now a natural instinct to time the arms and body to square the club direction to the target. Notice the shaft and clubhead riding down the right forearm. This indicates it is on plane at this moment.

The arms and body have now created a high amount of speed to square the club. The swing should feel very natural and free-flowing. The left side is holding resistance as the right side is now starting to widen the arc of the swing by straightening out. Both arms are being fully extended.

Release the entire swing toward the target. See the shaft now fully releasing the head of the club. The shaft should be pointing directly at the target, parallel to one of the straight line positions. The stomach should also start to point toward the target. It should all be about the target. The swing is often thought of as the motion in your body. It is most effective when working toward the target.

The spine angle is tilted for the final moment during a full swing. The shaft will form about a 45-degree angle. Looking at the clubface, the angle matches the shaft angle as it is released. This indicates that the clubface angle is square as it strikes the ball. The shaft is either on plane, as this photo shows, or it is not. It can only be steep or shallow. The clubface angle can only be square, open, or closed.

At the finish of the full driver swing, the shaft is sitting behind the ears, and the hands are near the left ear, as shown below. This is a full release of the body, arms, and hands, with the club holding its finish position. Look at how the right heel is on top of its toes and the weight is all the way on the front side. The right shoulder is now the closest to the target as the right side of the body is holding its momentum as you evaluate where the shot went.

Deliver the hit with the entire body. The rotation is what makes it possible for the straight shot. Look at the following sequences. See the loaded position from the downswing to impact. The arms and hands are in front of the stomach, and the hands and club are forming a straight line.

This first position on the downswing forms a "V" between the arm and in the shaft. This indicates the proper downswing transition. The weight is transferring from the push of the right leg and hip as it delivers the proper angle and sequence. This sequence of shifting the weight is what brings the club to the inside of the swing plane that is necessary for a powerful strike. Without this move, the next two moves would make it a weak sequence of motion. The right hip will create leverage by pushing, while the left side is receiving the loaded position and will build resistance for the next move.

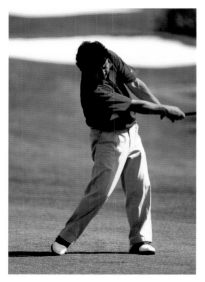

The rotation has been fully released at this point. Next, you must allow the arms to have speed. Also, allow them to move freely in front of the body. If the arms are not able to create speed through this position, that means that somewhere in the swing, they are getting stuck. You will need to find where you're stuck and fix the mechanics of the swing. A video of your swing can help you spot your error.

# Section IV

## The Dynamics of Driving

# DRIVER SWING VS. IRON SWING

## CHAPTER 9

There are significant differences between the driver swing and an iron swing. When you're swinging the driver, you must make a full shoulder turn and rotate all the way on the backswing. The full iron swing is a smaller version of a driver swing. It is no more than 75 percent of a driver swing on both sides of the swing.

At the top of the driver backswing, the hips, shoulders, and even your knees and feet move quite significantly away from the golf ball. In fact, the left heel should come off the ground to get the maximum turn in your backswing. And on the finish of your driver backswing, your entire back should be facing the target. In fact, your right shoulder will be closer to your target than your left shoulder. That is a good position to be in when you are at the completion of your backswing.

When you watch Jason Day and Adam Scott during the finish of their backswings, you will see them maximize the turn. They have a wider stance than normal. In fact, their setup stance is so wide that their feet are set outside their shoulders. It is necessary to swing as hard as you can and maintain balance and also to get a full coil on the backswing when you are driving the ball. When you are fully coiled on the follow-through, there is also a shift that takes place on both sides of the swing. On the backswing, the upper body coils above the right leg as much as possible while maintaining balance on the left leg. From there, the body shifts, and due to the feet being outside the shoulders, the body can move much more laterally and from there coil to the fullest extent, allowing it to move to the left side. With the momentum of the driver, the shoulders and arms will pass the golf ball; in fact, they will be 120 degrees on the follow-through.

On the follow-through, the right shoulder should be pointing at your target. One of the best ways to understand this is to watch Michelle Wie, who is one of the longest drivers on the

LPGA Tour. Watching her unwind her finish, you will see that during her swing, the right shoulder is pointing to the target.

These are some of the characteristics of an iron shot that are different from those of a driver shot. You're making an abbreviated backswing no more than about 75 percent of your full swing, and from there you're trying to push your right heel down into the ground when you follow through so that you can control the iron swing. On the follow-through, you'll see that the shoulders will have less movement toward your target, and the swing will be abbreviated through your finish.

Sometimes when you see players make a full iron swing, it's really a driver swing with the iron, to maximize the iron shot. They still don't get the same result of the driver swing, because when you hit a driver, your stance has a much wider base, and the speed of the club is much faster. So try to keep in mind that when you're using the iron (as opposed to the driver), the swing must be in control. Therefore, you do not have the full turn that goes into hitting with the driver.

During the driver swing, the shoulders must turn at least 90 degrees. In fact, if you turn more than that, it's not a bad thing to do. To allow that to happen, your hips have to be turning with the body while the left heel comes off the ground an inch. If you're not as flexible, it's okay to have your foot two to three inches off of the ground. This is okay, because that's how Jack Nicklaus got his full coil with his driver.

I believe that the left heel coming off of the ground is a natural instinct for a full coil. Today's players are trying to keep the left heel down while trying to use more resistance in the swing. This restricts the backswing and causes a lot of stress on the lower back. This is not necessarily a good move for average golfers. They do not have time to train their body to have this type of flexibility.

Also, during your driver swing, your head moves away from the ball slightly more than with an iron swing. This allows you to get farther behind the ball. This helps you to remain level on the backswing. Avoid a reverse pivot, which is moving your head toward the target.

On the forward swing, allow the right shoulder to turn all the way to 120 degrees or as far as possible. If you have to, open your left foot at setup while pointing it at the target to help you accomplish the full follow-through. Most tour players have their front foot open to get a maximum turn through the ball.

Lee Trevino, who also was a great ball striker, had his left foot pointed out toward the target every time he hit the golf ball. That allowed him to get through that ball without any resistance from his front leg. If your left heel is pointing closer to your target at address, when you go through the ball, you'll feel a lot of tension in your left leg and in your left foot. This will not allow a full turn of your shoulders on the follow-through. You can eliminate this by opening up the left foot at address.

When you're hitting the iron shot, you want accuracy and control. Your left foot should be less open than for a driver at setup. This will help you to limit that fullness in your follow-through and to stay more controlled. If you want to hit the ball farther, rather than swinging harder, move up a club, but keep using no more than 75 percent of your swing. This will allow the body to abbreviate on the follow-through so that the swing becomes more controlled. This is the biggest difference between an iron swing and a driver swing.

# SETUP FOR DRIVING SUCCESS

To set up the driver successfully, you have to have the correct fundamentals: ball position, head position, and your weight distribution behind the ball. These elements are important, because you're swinging the club differently (in terms of dynamics) than when you are swinging an iron. You are no longer swinging down on the ball like when you are hitting an iron. You are actually swinging up on the ball. So the ball position must be played off of the inside of your left foot. The only thing in line with the ball is your left ankle. The rest of your body is behind the ball. Let's do a step-by-step guide to set up for your drive so that it will be successful.

While standing in front of the ball with your feet two inches apart from each other, take your left foot and move it three to four inches toward the target. Next, take your right foot and move it all the way back to where both of your feet are now outside of your shoulders. The wide stance will help you to create a longer flat spot by the ball that will help you to drive the ball off the tee.

Your weight should favor the back foot at address. The weight distribution should be a minimum of 60 percent of your weight on your right foot. Position the weight properly, and your head and your upper body will be behind the ball. Your upper body needs to create an added tilt leaning toward your right side. Your right shoulder dips down much lower at setup than when you are setting up for an iron shot. When you do that, you'll notice that your head is tilted back behind the ball. If you draw a straight line from the ball to your body, the only things that will be in front of the golf ball are your left knee and ankle. At

this point, 90 percent of your body will be behind the golf ball. This will help you to set up for the driver. It helps you to create an ascending blow, so that you are swinging up at the ball.

From this address position, you will see from the corner of your eye the back end of the club. Now that you are in the correct position, be sure to move your feet and waggle the club so that you can get some movement before you begin your swing. Be sure that you are not staying stagnant at address. Feel the weight on the inside of your right foot by pinching the right knee inward. This also will help the weight to fall on your right side. Now, when you are making the backswing, the weight is already there for you to coil into. Make a full coil on the backswing so that you can push off that right side and are able to get the correct sequence of motion to get the correct downswing. Setting up for success is so important in driving the golf ball. You have to be positioned correctly so that you can be more consistent.

Repeat this step-by-step setup until you get it right. Set up over and over again so that this becomes a routine. This will help you to stay focused while driving the ball. So when you begin your address, be sure to go through these steps.

# LOSE CONTROL FOR TOTAL CONTROL

## CHAPTER 11

In order to drive the ball powerfully and effectively, you must swing fully and let go of trying to control your swing. Do not try to steer or control the ball in the direction where it is headed. Rather, trust that your setup and your swing are good enough to allow the ball to go to the target! Once you start your swing, you cannot try to manipulate it so that it goes straight. You must let go and trust that you have taken a good grip, posture, and stance and that all of these components are working together to produce the best possible shot. This cannot happen if you're trying to steer and manipulate your swing, because it will put tension on your golf swing. It will cause randomness to the point where you will miss more shots than you will hit good ones.

To get the feel of this, imagine that you are hitting the golf ball into a desert instead of a fairway that is composed of all kinds of obstacles. When you picture a big open space in front of you, there's no way you can miss that fairway. So if you trust that you can hit straight down the fairway, then you can swing freely and let the club and the ball do what they do without trying to make it happen.

A good drill to do is to swing the club in slow motion so that you can feel the positions in your swing. You can do this on the range and at home. You want to have that same feeling of moving through the positions of your swing when you're driving the ball off the tee. Taking a practice swing is also a necessary element in gaining control of your drive. Make sure that when you take a practice swing, it is hard enough to make a swooshing noise at the post-impact position on your left side. Be sure to hit off your front foot as you start to hit through the drive. This helps you to have full speed while going at the ball.

It is important to note that if you decelerate, you will lose control and all kinds of power. When you try to manipulate the club and steer your swing, you will slow down your swing and hit the golf ball instead of swinging through the ball. Without top speed going full throttle past the golf ball, you will not get the full follow-through and the feeling of full extension before finishing your swing.

Using full speed during your swing while letting go of control, you will gain accuracy and power all the way through the finish of your swing. When you are driving through the golf ball, you do not want to be hesitant on the follow-through. It is also true on the backswing. This is what you should be thinking when you're hitting the golf ball off the tee. Be sure when you finish your swing to feel the arms in a relaxed position. They should never be tight or tense. Relax your arms and let them fall over your left shoulder so that you finish with the arms bent and relaxed.

All of the extension and the full speed in your swing have already happened. The key is to come to a relaxed position in your finish. All of your weight is toward your left side facing the target. You can now evaluate your shot. This is the position you want to have on the finish of your swing.

During the swing, be sure that you are moving in an athletic and fluid manner so that all of the energy moves to the end of the golf club. If you finish your swing and you feel tension in your arms, the delivery of the power did not go to the club. Therefore, you are not getting maximum power.

# Section V

Mastering the Short Game

# PITCH SHOTS 12

## Pitch It Your Way

Most pitch shots require the club to load up to this halfway position. From here, you can hit most short pitch shots. Most important, after acquiring the skills to put the club in the correct position, its different speeds and the three locations of the follow-through will determine how far your ball will travel. Practicing these yardages is important, especially when you're playing on the course and are able to choose the right swing for the distance.

By placing your follow-through to each of the three different positions, you now can practice distance control. For me, the quarter distance is 25 yards, the half distance is 50 yards, and the three-quarter distance is 75 yards. For example, practice hitting a quarter shot follow-through, where the club is below the hands at the finish. Look at the photo below; it shows a quarter shot. The quarter shots will control a quarter of your distance. I hit my sand wedge 100 yards maximum distance. So, a quarter swing will go 25 yards in distance. This next photo shows the halfway follow-through, where the club is released above the hands. This will control a half distance 50-yard swing and three- quarter swing equal to 75 yards.

Keep in mind that all courses are different and your game needs to adapt to the conditions of the golf course, especially around the green. You need to answer questions such as, "How does my ball react after hitting the green from a quarter distance from the fairway? Or from the rough?" and "Is the green soft, and will the ball stop? Or is it hard, and will the ball roll out after

it hits?" Observing these reactions and knowing how to play these shots will give you the correct shot to get the ball close to the hole. You will need to master the feel for these positions.

## Setting Up for the Pitch

Pitch shots are executed with your normal swing, but by using a smaller version of it. Use your same swing while modifying the length of the swing and the width and angle of your stance, to control distance. This is the simple way to calculate how wide you should stand and how long your swing should be.

The shorter the distance, the narrower the stance should be. As you get farther away, the stance should get wider and the length of your swing should be longer. These two go hand in hand. The reason for this is that the lower body supports the leverage and length that the backswing travels and can be a foundation for the speed of your swings. When you stand with your feet too close together, it cannot produce great speed or power. In pitching the ball, this helps you to finesse your pitches rather than to overpower them. For example, imagine a power lifter or a baseball player or any other sports figure who needs leverage. The more power needed, the wider the stance should be. When a baseball batter goes to bunt the ball, his stance is narrow so he can hit the ball a short distance. When your stance is narrower, you can only support softer movements and slower speed, which is good for a golf shot that requires finesse. Try to swing hard with a narrow stance, and you'll find yourself falling off balance because it does not support the leverage. This is the simple way to determine how wide you should stand and how long your swing should be.

## Pitching Technique

Setting up properly is very important on all pitch shots. There are many ball positions and feet positions that you will have to get right to hit the proper shot. As I mentioned before, the narrow stance is for shorter pitch shots. The next thing to do is to open your stance. That means to point your toes toward the target.

## The Benefits of Hitting a Low Pitch

Hitting a low pitch shot is a great way to practice your wrist position at impact. The flat left wrist position or a slightly bowed left wrist position is a fundamental in golf. All great players have that one thing in common.

When the ball is on the ground, you must hit down on the ball in a descending blow. You strike down on the ball to take a divot. To do this, the hands must lead the leading edge of the club, forming a straight line from your shoulder to your wrist and the club shaft. Most of us can begin to practice this shot with a pitching wedge. Learn to hit the wedge low, as if you were de-lofting the pitching wedge into a 9 iron or an 9 iron loft. The ball will go farther than expected when you first practice this shot, as it will jump off the clubface. This helps amateur golfers to not add loft to the club by flipping it. The cupped left wrist position at impact will lose players distance and have an effect on consistency.

## Hit with a Flat Left Wrist

Practice your hit-and-hold pitch, finishing in the 4 o'clock position on the follow-through. This position with the flat left wrist will give you a great feel for impact. The right knee will move toward the target. The right wrist at this point will have increased in angle from where it was at the address, due to the resistance in the left wrist. You are trying to avoid flipping the club in a cupped left wrist position. This pronounced right wrist angle and the flat left wrist position allow the body to rotate to the ball. Keep the arms and club in front of you. The upper left arm should feel tight against the side of your torso. This represents the proper impact position. The clubface should always trail the hands. Practice this with a pitching wedge to feel the leading edge of the club strike the ball first, then the ground. If you do this correctly, you will feel the ball jumping off the clubface. It's a great feeling to have when you are struggling to make consistent contact with the ball.

In 1995, I learned the importance of this position when I worked at Oak Hill Country Club in Rochester, New York. As a young golf professional in my twenties, I was hired to help run the Ryder Cup for the Club. I was an assistant to Craig Harmon, who was the head pro at the time. During those years, I learned about the legendary player and instructor Claude Harmon. Craig was his son, and he passed down to me his father's teaching method. Claude would always say that the feeling of the left wrist should be as though there were a piece of steel running right through the wrist and forearm. This position creates a straight line. The point is that you should never bend your wrist or forearm during impact. After many years of learning and teaching golfers the hit-and-hold position, I agree that you must be able to execute this position successfully during your pitching swings. If you cannot achieve this in a pitch shot, then you most likely are not doing it in your full swing. Practice this over and over, so that the flat left wrist position becomes permanent in your swing. Isolating this drill where you hit and hold the flat left wrist position will help you make this position obtainable if you are struggling with cupping your left wrist at impact.

## High Pitch

High pitch shots can be played by adding loft to the club. How do you add loft and be consistent? There are many ways to play the flop shot.

After many years of watching, I often find high-handicappers failing to mimic professionals by opening the club and taking an exaggerated open stance and a full swing. Trying this type of lob shot is not the best option for average golfers.

The better way to hit the ball with a high pitch is by standing square or slightly open, by leaning the shaft back away from the target. You should not open the clubface; that makes the club point to the right of your target.

Looking down at the club, you can see that it is square to the target, as the shaft is leaning backward. This helps you to be more consistent in your swing by using the bounce of the club. The bounce of the club allows the club to slide under the ball with consistency.

The position of the ball is in the center of your stance or slightly forward. The weight is on the left side to ensure that your body will follow through to the finish. For more height in the shot, lean the shaft back away from the target while allowing the clubhead to lie square to the target. Next, get into the proper setup. First, place the club on the ground by leaning the shaft backward so that the clubface is facing up toward the sky. Second, grip the club and address the ball. This may feel awkward at first, but with practice, this becomes a simple method to control the height of the ball. This position will add plenty of loft to the club. During the swing, slide the back end of the club under the ball so it lands softly on the green.

## Control the Distance

This is not an absolute, but a guideline. Let's say that you hit a full swing wedge 100 yards. Now, as a rule of thumb, let's say you are 25 yards from the hole. The idea is to take a "quarter-of-the-distance" stance with your feet apart a quarter of the distance of your full stance. This allows you to swing comfortably a quarter of the length in each direction—meaning a quarter

of the way on the backswing and a quarter of the way in the follow-through.

Using your body as a clock, with the top of your head being at 12 o'clock and your feet being at 6 o'clock, a quarter of the way on the backswing would put your hands at 8 o'clock, and the follow-through would be at 4 o'clock. With the same rhythm of your swing, this would generally go 25 yards.

Now, let's say you are 50 yards from the hole. Take a stance with your feet apart half of the distance of your full stance. This allows you to swing half of the way in the backswing and half of the way in the follow-through. Using your body as a clock, the backswing would put your hands at 9 o'clock, and the follow-through would be at 3 o'clock. With the same rhythm of your swing, this would generally go 50 yards. It's because now you are getting your wrists involved, and once the wrists are hinged fully on both sides, it adds enough speed and leverage to be a half-swing. It's referred to as an L swing back and an L swing forward.

Next, let's say you are 75 yards from the hole. The idea is to take a stance with your feet apart three-quarters of the distance of your full stance. That allows you to swing three-quarters of the way in the backswing and three-quarters of the way in the follow-through. Using your body as a clock, the top of your head being at 12 o'clock and your feet being at 6 o'clock, three-quarters of a swing on the backswing would put your hands at 11 o'clock and 2 o'clock on the follow-through. With the same rhythm of your swing, this would generally go about 75 yards. This is a general description in how to control distance.

# Y vs. L Swing

## Y Swing

Use the Y swing on short pitches, typically 25 yards and closer to the hole. The Y that I am referring to is formed at address. The Y-to-Y swings back and through during this shot. Here is the reference point that you are looking for in the letter Y. The arms and the shaft form a letter Y shape as you look down to the ball. From the setup, take the Y back and through, maintaining that shape through all of the shot. This eliminates the wrist action in your swing. It allows you to control the shorter distance much better.

During the short swing, you will feel your upper body, especially your center and torso, moving together in one piece. That is what you're trying to accomplish, as you are eliminating the hands or the wrist action for this swing. Therefore, the ball is hit more softly and delicately on these short-distance pitch shots, providing control for the short distance. It is difficult to control short distances when there is a lot of wrist action. This encourages deceleration in your swing due to the power it loads up in the shaft. Too much wrist cock encourages deceleration in the short-distance pitches.

A good drill to practice the Y position swing is to place the butt end of the club to your stomach just below your belly button and grip down on the club. Your hands should be on the shaft. From there, swing the club back to the 4 o'clock position and then swing it forward to the 8 o'clock position. While doing this, your torso will move with the club, maintaining that connection between the butt end of the club and your stomach while the hips and knees finish toward the 8 o'clock position. The right knee will kick past the ball, and the ankle will roll forward; if the heel comes off the ground slightly, that is okay. This movement gives your body better control of the short shot.

Now, when you are hitting this shot, the Y-to-Y swing will allow the ball to hit softly on the green and roll like a putt. By

doing this, you will have a consistent shot to play around the green. Any added wrist action will put too much spin on the golf ball. In this case, with the backspin, the ball will react at random, depending on how it lands on the green. Sometimes the ball will land on the green and stop, while at other times it will continue rolling.

Most tour players prefer not to put backspin on short-distance shots. They prefer to have the ball land softly on the green and roll like a putt toward the hole. This is a more consistent way to play these shots. Remember to hold your club softly during the pitch so that you can feel the weight of the club. It will take some practice, but this shot will pay huge dividends, as you will be facing this shot many times in your round. When you master the Y-to-Y pitch, you will lower your handicap. The closer you pitch the ball near the hole, the better your chance in making your putt to get up and down from around the green.

## The L Swing

Use the L swing on pitch shots that are over 25 yards from the hole. The half swing will go about 50 yards and the three-quarter swing will go about 75 yards. Both of these shots require an L position on both sides. During this shot, the arm and the shaft form an L on the backswing and an L on the forward swing. Remember to swing with your regular rhythm as you would in a full swing, but be sure that you strike the ball first (and not the ground).

In order to make solid contact, the chest and your belt buckle must release toward your target on the follow-through. One of the biggest mistakes amateurs make is that they keep their chest facing the ball on the follow-through rather than releasing it toward the target. This is also true with your head position. Your head needs to turn toward the target. These are important tips to remember when you are struggling to make solid contact.

At the setup, your weight should be on the left side. During the backswing, there is no shifting of your weight. You continue holding it on the left side as you move through the impact position. At the finish, the weight is fully on your left side. This is something you should practice on the range to hone in on your distance. By monitoring your ball position and your clubface angle, you can control the height and distance depending on the shot you are trying to play. Be sure that there is a slight divot in front of the ball. If you are not taking a divot in front of the ball, you are likely not hitting these pitches with a descending blow to the ground.

# CHIP SHOTS

## Use Your Putting Stroke

Mastering the chip shot around the green is one of the fastest ways to lower your handicap.

When you are chipping, use your putting stance and stroke.

There are only two times when you stroke a golf ball—during putting and chipping. Setting up to chip the same way that you set up to putt is ideal. There are some differences in the ball position and in the weight distribution when you are comparing putting and chipping. Other than that, the way you stand over the address position should be very similar.

You can do this by standing over the ball with a putter and then switch to a chipping club. Use the same stroke with all of the chipping clubs. Land the ball approximately three feet onto the putting surface. When you switch to a lower-number club, the ball will roll out farther toward the hole.

As you set up to your chip shot with your pitching wedge, the club will feel longer than normal, and cramped. This is the correct feel for this position if you are doing it for the first time. To get more comfortable with this position, it will help you to offset the length by choking down on the club and holding the grip more in the palms of your hands. The club will lie along the lifeline of your hands. When you do this, you will bring the club's shaft in a more upright position, as you would do when using a putter.

This will bring the heel of the club's leading edge off of the ground. The toe of the club will be flush to the ground, while there will be air under the heel of the club. This is what you are trying to achieve—heel up with the toe down.

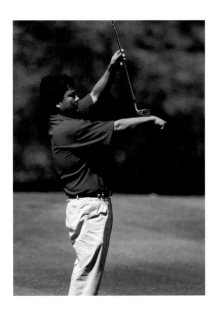

One of the most common misses in chipping is catching the heel of the club on grass, causing you to stub the shot. It stops the momentum of the club from sliding through the grass. Keeping the toe down and the heel up will slide the club through for a smooth chip. By sitting the bottom of the club correctly on the ground, your chip shot will have a greater chance for success, thus giving you confidence in your stroke. Catching the heel on the grass can cause you to be inconsistent in distance control and to ruin an opportunity to get the ball up and down from around the green.

When you set up for a chip shot, the ball position should be toward the back foot. The shaft of the club will be leaning forward. The clubhead will be in line with your back foot, and the grip will be in line with your left thigh. This will guarantee the correct shaft position in your setup for a successful chip. Your hands will be ahead of the clubface to ensure you make solid contact with the ball.

Some professional players have been known to use the same grip when chipping as they do when they are putting. The most commonly used grip in putting is the reverse overlap. This grip allows the right hand to control distance. Practice this grip and see if it works for you to determine whether or not using it on the course during your round would be a good choice.

When the ball sits on the collar of the green with a good lie, it can be played off your right toe or even more inside your stance. If the lie is flat, you will not need to lean forward as much on the front foot. You can stand over the ball with the weight evenly distributed 50-50 on both sides. Depending on where the hole is located at the start of the green, the distance from your ball to the hole on the target line will determine your club selection. I will discuss "the three-club system" later on, so that you can select the best club for the shot you will be making.

When a ball is sitting in a good lie and presents a level stance, you can set up just like a putt in a chipping stance. The worse the lie is, the more you will need to play the ball back in your stance toward the right toe. By playing the ball farther back in your stance, the shaft lean will increase, pushing the hands forward. The weight distribution will favor your left side. Depending on the lie, it can be as much as 80 percent on the left foot and 20 percent on the right foot. Remember the club position when you look down; it should consistently line up with your left thigh. So the farther the ball position is played back in your stance, the more lean you will have in the club. Again, this is mostly influenced by the difficulty of the lie position.

When the ball sits down in a difficult lie, such as higher grass, you will need to place the ball off the right foot. Depending on the severity of the lie, you can play the ball back outside of the right foot. Remember, the farther you play the ball back, the more lean you will have in the shaft of the club. The weight distribution will favor the front foot. More important, it will change the dynamics of the stroke from being more level to a steeper downswing.

On even lies, with the ball position off the right toe, a simple putting stroke can be used. It should feel just like a putt with limited play in the wrist. But, when you are playing the ball farther back in the stance, you will have to increase the shaft angle at address. The club will come up more on the backswing in a sharper arc due to the setup. You will hit down on the ground more and feel more resistance in your follow-through. The club is now hitting the ball more sharply and thus deeper into the ground. When you hit this shot with the correct setup, you will catch the ball clean and get the ball out more consistently. This will help you control distance much better because you will hit the ball more cleanly.

When you are faced with uneven lies, be sure to place your weight distribution with the slope of the lie and to swing with the slope. For example, the downhill lie de-lofts the club, and the ball coming off the club is firmer. It will fly lower and roll out more once it hits the green. The weight distribution will favor the left side at the setup. You are now swinging with the downhill slope. In this situation, take a lesser club. A downhill lie can influence the ball to push out to the right.

The uphill lie adds loft to the club, so the ball coming off the club is softer. It will fly higher and roll out less once it hits the green. The weight distribution will be favoring the right side at the setup. You are now swinging with the uphill slope. In this situation, take more club. An uphill lie can influence the ball, pulling it to the left.

When the ball is above your feet, your weight will be more on the heels of your feet. It is the opposite of when you play the ball below your feet. When the ball is below your feet, your weight will be more on your toes. This means that the ball will push out to the right. It is never a good idea to work against the slope at address or during the swing. Be sure to offset the differences in your setup by selecting the correct club and aiming correctly, knowing the effect that the slopes will have on your stroke.

## Hands Off

To play the chip shots correctly, and to use the correct technique, you must limit the involvement of hands in the stroke. It is the same as adding hands during your putting stroke in that it affects the distance control.

Distance control is very important in chipping around the green. First, you must learn to make solid contact by using the right fundamentals and technique in the stroke. Standing close to the golf ball, as you do when you are putting, will help you to make your stroke more vertical. Taking your club straight back and straight through are key things to remember when you're stroking your chip shots.

Next, it's really important for your shoulders to create a pendulum motion when chipping. This means that on the backswing, your shoulders should move like a pendulum. The left shoulder dips down on the backswing as the right shoulder goes up. This shoulder movement reverses as you go forward: the right shoulder dips down and the left shoulder pulls up.

During your chip shots, you do not want the shoulders to rotate. It's the same principle as the putting stroke, except you are hitting off your front foot. To get the right feel, you must rock your shoulders back and through so there really are no hands involved in the stroke. On the backstroke, you want to feel that the clubface doesn't have any rotation. The clubface stays square; it will feel like you're taking the club and closing it down slightly. The club stays on a straight line as it goes back and through the swing. If you follow these principles, you will make chipping simple.

One way to practice this is to put a shaft underneath both your arms just above your elbows and up against your chest. Next, allow the shaft on the backswing and the forward swing to go straight down and straight up so that the shoulders are rocking. Do not let that shaft rotate behind you to the right or to the left. This is a good drill to help you with the proper chipping technique.

If your shoulders are moving properly during your chipping stroke, you will hit the center of the clubface almost every time during your chip. Keep in mind that your weight does not shift

to the right or left during your chip shot. You are holding your weight in the same position as when you started. The right knee does kick forward toward the ball at this point.

Another good drill to get this feel is to lay two clubs down on the ground like a railroad track. Next, put the ball in the middle of the clubs. Make sure that it is pointing at your target. Then, square up or set up slightly open to the chip and allow the club to go back and through on that track. At the top of your stroke, where the club is approximately three to four feet away from the ball, you should still see the club on the track. As you go through after you make contact and on the finish of your chip shots, you should still see the club on that track. When you accomplish this in your chipping, you will have mastered a very simple move that will stand the test of time. It will help you to achieve solid contact with the proper stroke that will keep the ball on target.

Seve Ballesteros was one of the all-time best short game players. He chipped this way. He always kept his elbows soft and slightly bent. He also bent over more than usual. Seve would make a simple stroke back and through, never flipping his wrists. This allowed the arms and shoulders to work together. These are some of his secrets that he shared, which made him one of the finest short game players in the world.

It is also ideal to release your head on the follow-through as you chip. Do not keep your head still. It's important to have freedom so that your head moves with the shoulders' release while going to the follow-through. This helps you to hit the ball consistently in the center of the clubface each and every time. Keeping the eyes and head down at the ball restricts your follow-through. There has been way too much talk about keeping the head still. The best players have always had that subtle movement forward that kept them fluid in their stroke.

At the setup, your shaft leans forward, thus making your left wrist flat and creating a pronounced angle on your right wrist. The angle of your right wrist is fully hinged at this position. The left wrist is flat and does not change on your backstroke, at impact, or during your forward stroke. If you maintain the same angle in your hands, the only way to move the club back will be with your shoulders rocking backward and forward. The distance between the elbows remains the same. So, from your setup, the angles that you create from the shaft of the club that go all the way up to your wrist and your arms do not change throughout the entire stroke.

Too many golfers rotate their shoulders on the backswing. This sucks the club inside, and you will hit behind the ball or you will skull the ball. This happens because it's too hard to make a correction on such a short stroke. Typically, the club path goes too far inside when you use too much wrist in your stroke. You must keep the club in front of you. Remember, when you are chipping, you do not want the club to have any rotation throughout the stroke. The club should go straight back and straight through, keeping the hands passive during the chip.

## The Three-Club System

There are many ways to hit a chip shot. This is one of the things that professional golfers do very well. They use a system that allows one stroke and one specific landing area.

My three-club system is a method that gives you a reference point to use around the green for every chip shot. You will choose the appropriate club depending on how far your ball is from the hole.

In order to use this system, you must first learn that there's one spot that you want to hit on the green during a particular shot. That spot is the same place for every shot that you are trying to hit to. You may have noticed that professional golfers usually walk around the green before their chip shot. They evaluate their chip shot so that they can look for the best place for their ball to land. It is necessary that your ball land in a specific spot where it will roll down to the hole. This is very similar to putting.

The landing area that you are looking for is a spot about three feet past the fringe on the green. Make sure that your club is on your target line. This is crucial, because this determines where the ball will curve on the putting surface. After your shot lands, it will be in the desired place and in position to putt.

Once you have identified the three-foot spot on the putting surface, the next question that you must ask is, "How far does the ball need to travel to get to the hole?" Once you have evaluated both of these distances, then you can use the three-club system to figure out what the best option is for your shot.

The three clubs that we use in my system are a pitching wedge, a 9 iron, and a 7 iron. The equation for using these clubs is as follows:

The pitching wedge is used for loft. The pitching wedge controls about the same distance in the air as on the ground. This is the rule of thumb that you will need to use, especially when you are practicing this shot. When using your pitching wedge, you will get into your chipping stance. While stroking back, keep an even pace and make sure your hands and arms are soft. This will allow the shoulders to control the stroke.

Always remember that when you are chipping to your desired spot, once you have identified the line and the direction of that exact spot on the green, the ball needs to hit the green and then roll to the hole. There is no need to look at the hole, but practice that same stroke before you take your shot. It is best to avoid looking at the flagstick, too. This is to prevent the body from reacting to the flagstick, as opposed to the actual target (the hole).

Look at that spot on the green where you want your ball to hit; this will allow you to feel the stroke in the direction of your shot. When practicing, learn to focus on your target while checking your stroke. This allows the club to effectively do what it's designed to do. It will take some practice to evaluate your chip and to figure out where your landing area is on the green. The landing area you want to target is always three feet past the fringe on the green. This gives you enough space between the fringe and the green, so that you can comfortably hit to your target. Remember, when you're around the green, it's easier to make a smaller stroke that you can hit a longer distance.

The main reason why you are picking a landing area that is close to you is that it is a more consistent shot. Professionals prefer this shot, because they typically have to take the shot under a lot of pressure. This is a much simpler way to make the shot a success.

Picking the right line for your putt is the next step. If you have a putt that will break six feet to the left once it hits that spot, considering that the green has a consistent one-way break in the slope, you would aim six feet to the right of the straight line to your target line. This is because, as you would with a putt, you have to play the break once the ball rolls on the ground. For this shot, use a pitching wedge and land the ball three feet on the putting surface and six feet to the right of your direct target line. Now, you have successfully chosen an exact landing area for your shot.

The second club you will be using is a 9 iron. This club will allow you to hit the ball in the air one-third of the total distance to the target. Again, your landing area will be three feet onto the putting surface, and the remaining two-thirds of the distance will be the roll on the green toward the hole. Using the same stroke that you've used with your pitching wedge, get the ball to that three-foot spot on the putting surface. This club allows the ball to roll out farther than the pitching wedge. This means that the pitch shot for this club is used when the hole is farther away from the landing spot on the green. Remember, the total distance is two-thirds on the ground.

The best way to determine the distance is to walk up to the middle of the total distance that you have on the chip shot. Next, evaluate your shot from the side, looking at the total distance from the hole. It is never a good idea to evaluate your shot looking straight down the line from behind your ball. If the distance in the air equals the one-third of the way to the spot you're trying to hit and the remaining two-thirds is the roll to the hole, a 9 iron is your optimal club for the shot.

Now, let's discuss the third club in my system—your 7 iron. The ball will travel in the air one-quarter of the distance to achieve that three-foot spot on the putting surface. Remember that the three-foot spot stays consistent no matter which of the three clubs you are using during a chip shot. After evaluating the shot from the side, if a quarter of the distance is in the air to get to the spot on the green and three-quarters of the distance from that spot is the roll to the hole, the 7 iron is your best club to use. Remember to keep the ball position and stroke the same as you did with both the pitching wedge and the 9 iron. Allow the club to swing naturally.

There is a difference in the way in which the ball will travel when you use each of these three clubs. The pitching wedge will pop the ball up a little bit higher and land more softly. It will roll an equal distance on the ground as it flies in the air. With the 9 iron, the ball will travel mid-height in the air, a little lower than with the pitching wedge. Then, it will hit the spot that's one-third of the distance of the total distance of the shot. The ball will land at the three-foot spot on the putting green, before hitting and rolling two-thirds of the distance on the ground.

The 7 iron will be traveling at the lowest height of the three clubs. Once it hits that three-foot spot on the green, it will roll just like a putt, because you will be using a putting stroke. You will be using your putting stance, and the ball will only pop up because of the club's loft, and as it hits the green, it will roll three-quarters of the distance on the ground. The 7 iron should be the maximum club you should use to control the farthest distance that you may have for a chip shot. If you have a distance from the landing area farther than from that three-foot spot, you could play the ball slightly back in your stance to increase the roll. It takes practice around the green to control your distances. It is very rare that you would have a shot where you would have to roll the ball more than three-quarters of the distance to the hole, as most greens are not big enough to justify this special shot.

If you are faced with a long-distance chip due to an extra large and gimmicky green, you can play the ball back toward the back foot. You will still need to hit the three-foot spot on the green, but you should allow the ball to roll farther toward the hole. You would only use the 7 iron to get more distance.

The key to using my three-club system is to learn to evaluate where your landing area is on the green and the rest of the distance on the ground to the hole, and to decide what club is the best option. With my three-club system, you should be sure to pick the right line for your chip shot. Once it hits that spot, ask yourself: What will the ball do when it rolls out toward the hole?

Will it curve left or right? Will it go uphill? Once you have gone through the preliminary evaluation process and understand where these positions are and how the shot will play out, you can pick the best option. When you learn to evaluate like a pro, you will save strokes around the green, lowering your handicap. This is one of the fastest ways to save strokes on your score.

The next time you are on the golf course and are about to hit a chip shot, look for that three-foot spot on the putting green.

# PUTTING 14

## Personalize Your Style

Your putting stance should be comfortable for you. Remember to get your eyes over the ball and near the line of the putt. Your left eye should be directly above the ball, since the ball position should be in the front of the stance. The ball is in line with the inside of the left foot. Then the weight from this position should be 50 percent–50 percent while favoring the left side just a little bit. The weight is on the inside of the feet.

This is one of the ways to check if your eyes are in the correct position. I will say that this is more important in putting, since you are trusting your eyes to make every putt. To be a good putter, start training your eyes to have proper alignment. There is not much to the stroke, but being accurate in seeing the line helps when you want to make putts. Visualizing the target line will help you to make sure the putter face is even with the ground.

Hold the club with the right hand, and begin hitting the putts with one hand only. If you have never hit a putt before, this drill will help you establish a great feel for the concept that it doesn't take much to get the ball moving. It is more important to learn how to hit the center of the clubface with each putt. It looks easy, but it has its challenges.

Do a one-handed drill with the right hand and practice hitting the center of the clubface on each putt, as shown on page 141. Do this on six- to eight-foot putts, and be sure the movement of the putter is minimal and compact.

It is necessary to focus on being in a comfortable position when you're setting up the putt. When addressing the ball, you can find a relaxed position by bending over at your waist

and letting your arms hang down from your shoulders. While keeping your arms soft, you should hold the club in your hands softly. On a scale from 1 to 10 to measure the tension of the grip (1 being the softest), it should be a 2.

Putting is an art, not an exact science. Usually, instead of making major changes to my students' putting technique, I try to change the way they see putting so that they become confident with their own style. I am able to do this by getting them to relax physically and mentally before they putt. This helps them to be more confident with their putting. Confidence is a huge factor in being a great putter!

The flow can come from trusting yourself and getting in your mind that everyone can visualize the path to performing a good putting stroke. Being too mechanical can cause tension and block the flow that comes from being relaxed and allowing the putting stroke to perform.

To find your best putting stroke, you must be in a relaxed state physically and mentally as you set up over the golf ball. No matter what your preference is when you are setting up to putt, whether your stance is wide or narrow, or closed or open, keep in mind that it does not matter how you look over a putt. It is the most individual thing you do in golf. It's like your own signature—you must own your own style; do not borrow someone else's. Remember to apply some of the fundamentals that are discussed later in the book. They will help you to improve and become the best putter that you can be.

The ball must hit the center of the putter consistently if you want to become a great putter. I am always surprised during putting lessons how amateurs miss the sweet spot on their putter. If you don't hit the sweet spot, you lose distance control. Controlling speed is the most important part of putting.

Jack Nicklaus had a unique style to his putting. He crowded the ball and bent down low to the ground. When he was the best player in the world, I wanted to putt just like him. I putted this way during my high school years and putted well. Copying this style helped me to see the line of my putt easier. I was especially good from short distances, but I struggled on the long putts. Copying this style helped me briefly, but I knew I had to find my own personal style that could help me be a good putter from all distances.

I saw Ben Crenshaw putt one day while watching the Honda Classic in Ft. Lauderdale at The TPC at Eagle Trace. He stood over the ball tall and was almost the complete opposite of Nicklaus. I went and tried that after returning from the tournament at Martin County Golf Course, where I had practiced. This also was short-lived, as I improved my long putts, but then I could not putt the short putts well. This sent me out to search for something that would fit my style. Something in between the two players was what I needed. One of the things that made me a better putter was to stop trying to copy other styles of putting. I followed some basic fundamentals that allowed me to make more putts day in and day out.

I've experimented with many different ways in order to become a better putter. When the long putters came out, I tried using one during a tournament. Tournaments are the final frontier in knowing if the putt will hold up under pressure. During the middle of the round, I stubbed the long putter on the ground. Needless to say, I never played with one again.

It wasn't until later in my professional career that I found comfort in my own style of putting. This gave me confidence in my putting. I focused simply on finding the right line and the correct speed and trusted myself. This was the turning point in my putting. You can find your own way following the key fundamentals and by keeping putting simple.

Today, another style of putting that is producing good putters is the cross-handed putting grip. With this grip, the idea is to grip the club by reversing your hands. The left hand on this grip is lower on the club while the right hand is on the top. Jordan Spieth, one of the best players on tour today, has won two major championships using this style of putting grip. He putted better than anyone during the 2015 PGA Tour. There are many other younger players who are now being taught this style of putting stroke. They are following the example of Jim Furyk, who is a pioneer on the PGA Tour, for this style.

Jim Furyk started putting this way when he first learned to play golf. His father was a golf professional who taught him this style from the beginning. This works for Jim Furyk and Jordan Spieth, and it may work for you.

The left-hand low putting grip promotes a better swinging action with the leading arm and the shoulder. It helps to keep the clubface square through impact. This is a non-conventional grip. You will need time to adapt to this putting style, because any change that you make will feel uncomfortable at first. Changing your putting style is no different from making a swing change.

The other grip is the claw grip, which is popular among golfers. The claw grip refers to the position of the right hand. With this grip, the palm of your right hand is on top of the putter. To use this grip, you place the putter in between the forefinger and the thumb. This allows the putter to go back and through with limited face rotation in the putter.

This style has helped many golfers to overcome their yips.

## Distance Control

It's important to focus on the distance during all of your putts. This should remain a top priority on long-distance putts, as well. The speed of a putt changes when you play different courses. It is important to understand the speed on the putting green prior to playing the course. Practicing on the putting green before you go out onto the course is a must.

There are some really good drills to get a feel for the greens. The one-handed focus drill is one of the most effective and best ways to learn to control a long-distance putt. To do this drill, you hold the club with your right hand only. Then you swing the club like a pendulum hitting a long-distance putt. This drill allows the club to move in an uninterrupted manner. When you are hitting the putt in the center of the club every time, you will know how far the ball is going to go each time. When you miss the center of the putter, you will leave the putt short.

Once you've learned how to do this back and forth and you've gotten the pendulum feel, put the left hand on the club. Be loose and free with a lot of hinging on the backstroke. On the forward swing, let the putter go. The arms and the shoulders will work as one piece. When you have a long putt, you will need to be longer on the backstroke and shorter on the follow-through. It's the opposite for shorter putts. Make sure to allow the putter to have more follow-through.

Distance is important on all putts. It is very important to avoid three-putting on long-distance putts. While it is great to be a good short-distance putter, you will find that once you take yourself outside of the three- to five-foot range around the hole, your chances of making the putt will drop significantly.

Make sure you are taking practice putts on the putting green before you play! Hit a few putts with your right hand without aiming at a hole. Hit a few long putts from one side of the green to the other. Next, hit some shorter putts from side to side. Then finish with much shorter putts. Play the edge of the greens from one side to the next; make it about 40 to 45 feet for the putt.

The "Focus Towel" drill is another good drill to practice for controlling distance. Pick a small hand towel and lay it on the putting green. From 30 to 40 feet away, try to land the ball in the towel. This will help you to focus on landing the ball on a particular spot. The towel drill works well because it is above the green, and you can see something that's above the green better then you can a hole.

No matter what type of stroke you choose when putting, there are a few key things to remember. The ball position at setup is very important. Your eyes should be directly over the golf ball. Remember to try to keep your eyes parallel to your target line. Be sure that you are looking down the line to the hole. The ball should be in line with the inside of your left heel. Keeping your weight slightly left will help you to restrict any movement during your stroke.

A good way to check where your eye is in relationship to the ball is to take a ball and drop it from the level of your left eye. Wherever your ball lands, this is where it should be placed at address. It's not a bad idea to have your right knee slightly kicked inside your feet to maintain a stable position. If you are a release stroke putter, it's better to keep your weight over your feet at a 50-50 ratio. With your eyes directly over the ball line, it will help you to see the line of the target and the direction of your putt.

This is one of the things that helps me to improve my putting. When I'm not putting well, my eyes are not over the ball. This causes a misdirection of the putt, and it creates bad habits of pushing or pulling to steer the direction of the ball. I like to have my weight on the left side at address. I am more of a release putter. Whatever technique works for you, be sure to follow the fundamentals and keep your eyes over the ball and the ball position off the inside of your left foot.

## The Release or Block Stroke

The front view shows a squared setup with a position of balanced weight distribution. The hands are directly over the ball with the grip pressure soft. Both feet are parallel to each other. The knees slightly bent should give you a good feeling as you set up over the putt. The ball is slightly in the front of the stance so that the putt can be struck slightly on the upswing. This helps the ball to lift and roll out smoothly.

Just as the backstroke is executed mostly with the shoulders, notice the forearms, where the elbows are, and you'll see that the hands are in the same exact positions as they were from the setup. The pendulum motion of the shoulders is now taking them back. At this point, the left shoulder will dip under its original plane slightly, but it does not mean that it is actually doing so. The feeling of this sensation allows the stroke to be more repeatable.

As you hit your putt, it is important to keep the putter low to the ground as you follow through. The release of the putting stroke, when you keep the butt end of the putter pointing at the center of the body while the head of the club releases, allows the club to stay low. The follow-through should not be too long. The body should remain somewhat quiet, and the eyes should be quiet, as well. Try not to make sudden movements.

The release stroke and the block stroke are the two techniques that all golfers use. Jordan Spieth and Tiger Woods are two of the best release putters, while Ben Crenshaw and Phil Mickelson are two of the best block putters. These two different techniques have won many major championships. Neither of these two techniques is superior: it is a matter of choice.

A release stroke is defined as the putter head passing the butt end of a golf club after impact. You need to keep a center point that the butt end of a golf club has established at address. The best way to describe a release stroke putt is to go back to a putter that has now been banned from competition. It is the anchor putter. The anchor putter is pressed up against your body so that the putter can swing in a pure pendulum. This style of putting is now considered cheating according to the rules of golf.

The conventional way of executing the release stroke is to allow the putter head to pass the hands after impact. Keep the putter in between the forearms, evenly distributed at address. Both thumbs are straight down the shaft, where the palms face each other. The grip pressure is much lighter on the club. The typical missed putt is a pull.

The block stroke putters, such as Phil Mickelson and Ben Crenshaw, are some of the best putters who have ever played the game of golf. The block putters have a straight line from their shoulders all the way down to the shaft of the club. The putter head will not pass the hands after impact. It's a one-piece stroke going back and through the putt. They have their hands more in front of the clubface than the release putters at address. The left thumb is on the left side of the grip. This weak left hand position keeps the hands passive. It allows the shoulders to be in control. One of the drawbacks that I've seen in pros and amateurs alike is that they hold their putters too tightly in their hands. The tendency on the missed putt is a push.

No matter what type of stroke you choose, the fundamentals remain the same. Most important, keep your eyes over the ball. Also, play the ball off the inside of your left foot for the best results. These are your checkpoints that will help you to be a better putter.

## Commit, Commit, Commit

The following are some of the most important things to remember when you are learning how to take your putting to the next level. You must learn to trust and commit to your stroke no matter what line you have chosen to the hole. The key is to trust that you have evaluated and made the best decision on which line to start your ball. Next, decide how hard to stroke the ball. Then, trust your stroke and commit to all the decisions that you have made to give yourself a 100 percent chance of making the putt.

No putt is guaranteed to go in the hole. There are too many variables when you are putting. For example, the type of grass you are putting on and how it grows. Another one is the condition of the green, meaning how many bumps and spike marks your ball will have to go over while traveling to the hole. No matter what is in front of you, everyone is dealing with similar situations. The one thing you can control is making yourself commit to every putt. This will allow you to have the best chance at making the putt.

These are the characteristics of every great putter that has ever played the game. They understand that there is only so much of the outcome that they can control. The part that they can control is that they must roll the putt on the right line and hit it as solidly as possible with the best stroke possible. If you have done this, then you should be happy with your putt.

As I have mentioned, you must learn to pick a line and understand the break of the green. That is to say, which way the ball is going to turn as it approaches the hole. You need to ask yourself if the putt is a single-breaking or a multiple-breaking putt. When reading the green, look for the high points and low points. These will have the most influence on the break of the putt. Bermuda greens that are predominantly found in warm climates are grainy and can move the ball. There are many other things that influence the movement on the green.

Reading the green can be complicated, but you can make it as simple as possible. One of the ways that I have found that helps me to read the green is to walk around and feel the putting surface with my feet. So the next time you are looking at your putt and you are having a hard time determining the break, walk the line of your putt. You will feel the break or the hill that you can't see with your eyes. This is the reason why you see tour players walking around the hole. Not only are they getting a read from different angles, but also they are feeling around the hole with their feet for confirmation of the break of the putt. Try this the next time you are on the golf course.

Golf is one of the few sports in which your eyes stare at the ball when striking it. In a lot of other sports, you look at the target while executing the shot. Most of us are taught to keep our head and eyes focused on the ball at address and while striking the ball. It is the opposite in other sports, such as basketball: you are shooting while looking at the target.

Many golfers have tried putting the ball while looking at the hole. Sam Snead tried putting this way. He used a croquet-style putt through his legs and to the side. It was odd for the time period, and it was even weirder to see someone like Sam Snead using this type of putting stroke. It worked fairly well for him, but I don't think it worked well enough to convince the public that this was the new way to putt. Golf has a moment before you strike the ball, a few seconds of taking the eyes off the target as you stare at the ball just before you strike. Stare at the ball too long, and you will tense up and miss the shot. I tried the Sam Snead way of putting while looking at the hole. It worked well on occasion, but I could not trust it during tournaments. I will say that I never gave myself enough time to master this technique.

Now let's talk about the best player in 2015! With two major championship wins and a number-one ranking, Jordan Spieth has erased all of the doubts that you could win with this style of putting. He won big! His putting is what he did better than anyone on the planet that year. His putting is undoubtedly the best part of his game. He stared at the hole while striking his putts, and he even gripped the club in an unorthodox way by holding it cross-handed, which is a reverse overlapping grip. This caught the attention of the golf world. So, is his way of staring at the target while putting a better way, or is it something that works well just for him? Again, I believe it is a preference.

In the summer of 2001, I was playing in the Maine Open Championship in Portland, Maine. I was playing well heading into that week. I wanted to win the championship badly and needed to, because I was running low on money. I was hitting the ball well, and I knew that if I putted well, I had a good chance of winning the championship. During the practice rounds after I finished up with my round of golf, I would hit hundreds of putts before heading back to my hotel for the night. I was so determined to put in extra time and effort to get the results that I put a lot of pressure on myself to win.

Imagine the worst outcome, because that's what happened. I putted the worst that I had ever putted in a golf tournament. I replayed the round in my head to figure out what went wrong. As I got to thinking about it, I realized I had put too much pressure on myself every time I stepped foot on the green. I forgot to relax my mind and body before my putts. The more I applied pressure on myself, the worse I putted.

The lesson that I learned walking away from that tournament was to not set expectations for winning. The less you care when you stand over the ball and stroke it, the better you perform. I learned to put performance ahead of the results. You can't control the outcome. When you try to do this, tension sets in. Tension is the biggest killer of performance. Caring less will release tension, and it will allow you to putt your best.

# Section VI

Specialty Shots

## Three dos and don'ts

Fear goes away almost completely when a player understands how to hit the bunker shot. First, the sand wedge is the only club in your golf bag designed differently. It has an added weight on the back of the club, giving it a slide factor when used properly. This added weight is called the bounce. Just as it sounds, this club should bounce when used. This only happens with the proper setup. From the address position in the bunker, I drew two lines as an example. The ball is in the center of the 12-inch space between the lines, each of which is lined up with the inside of the foot. This is because in a proper bunker shot, the club should slide through the first line to the next. The ball position should be in the front of the stance next to the left heel. The club should be slightly open so that the bottom of the club can slide through.

The stance is wider than in a normal pitch shot. Most greenside bunkers are played best with a wider stance to help shallow the swing arc. This is so that the club can slide under the sand. The club only hits the sand. The thrust from the sand is what lifts the ball up and out of the sand. The swing has to be slightly longer, because you are not hitting the ball at all at this point. A full swing is encouraged, as most of your weight is going to be leaning on the left side as you swing.

One of the biggest challenges in the greenside bunker that I've seen for amateur golfers is created when they are taught to hit down in the sand and blast their way out! This is the opposite of how the pros approach these bunker shots. This technique can be dangerous, because you're swinging so hard. It appears that the pros are doing that, but one of the things that I recommend is that you avoid overswinging. The pros do not overswing out of the bunker. If you overswing trying to blast the sand, you may be setting yourself up for a disastrous result when you catch the ball first. The ball will rocket out of the bunker and out of play.

Focus on the right-hand-only drill. It is one of the best drills for your bunker swing. This is because you are using the release hand, which allows the club to splash the sand and slide the bottom of the club. Keep in mind that you cannot swing extremely hard with just the one hand, and it will help you to take less sand when you are using this swing to get the ball out.

In this section, I will share with you my focus drills that will help you to get out of the bunker with one swing every time. Without this urge to swing hard, you can get out of the bunker with ease.

Dos:

1.  Focus on your hand position, making sure it is even with or slightly behind the clubface. To begin with, have the shaft 90 degrees in front of your hands. This is a good position from which we can utilize the balance of the golf club. The ball position should be slightly forward in your stance, with the shaft even farther behind you. The face of the club is now in front of your hands. This will allow the club to slide under in a much shallower position. The feeling that you want is to let the club slide under thin, like the thickness of a dollar bill, as you go through the ball. This is because you are allowing the golf club to hinge on the backswing so that you're going to get the steepness that you're looking for, but you're trying to create more of a sliding action to shallow out your angle. That is a better way to get out of the greenside bunker.

    I prefer to do it this way rather than trying to get the golf club to fan open too much. Then you have to stand too far open in your stance. If your hands are in the correct position and the shaft points more behind you, the clubface will point to the sky with a lot more loft than you would originally have had if you put it straight down touching the leading edge. So if you place the balance of the club down to the ground and have the shaft almost feel as though you're pointing it toward your inside right hip pocket, then the ball position should be forward in line with your left heel. That's going to guarantee that the golf club will hit sand first, remaining in the sand for the distance of about a foot. Again, it is better to take your normal grip and try not to open the clubface but allow the shaft to lean back. That's the better way to hit your bunker shot.

2.  Your weight distribution is also very important when hitting a correct bunker shot. You should place the top half of the body in the center of your feet with just a slight bit of weight forward. Your upper body should be more level,

because you want the golf club to have a sliding motion. Your lower body will feel as though it's leaning toward your left side, but your upper body needs to be leaning toward the inside of your right foot. This is the feeling you want as you get into the proper setup. The last thing that you want is to lean too far forward with both your upper body and lower body, causing a steep angle into the golf ball. Remember, you're hitting down, but you're trying to create a more shallow impact through the golf ball so that the club has no interruption. Make sure you allow the bounce of the club to work to its fullest.

3. Taking the club back properly is a must as you execute this bunker shot. Having the club more in front of your hands as you go back and through your swing is very important. The feeling of the club as it goes back will hinge more quickly on the backswing. The visual picture is that the face of the club is still facing skyward as it goes through the ball. When you do this, you are releasing the club properly. When you are at your setup, your left hand should feel a little bit of a cock position. What you are trying to do is to increase that position on the backswing, with both hands hinging the club properly. This is the only time you're not trying to hit the golf ball first. So allow the lower body to remain quiet, and allow the golf club to pass your hands and then fully release to your finish. On smaller shots, your right heel can stay very quiet to where the heel comes off just a slight bit.

Don'ts:
1. One of the things to avoid in your setup during a bunker shot is having the shaft of the club lean forward with your hands in front of the clubface. When this happens, either you are playing the ball too far back in your stance or lunging forward with the upper body. When you are in this position, the leading edge of the club will dig into the sand. The other thing that will happen is that you will catch the

ball first, instead of catching the sand first. It also de-lofts the club angle. From this position of the clubface, it will be almost impossible to get enough height to clear a bunker with a high lip. This will make you try to compensate and in turn acquire the bad habit of trying to lift the ball in the air rather than allowing the club to do the work.

2.   The other position you want to avoid is having your head and the center of your body in front of the golf ball. This goes hand-in-hand with having the shaft and hands forward. Be sure that you set up properly to avoid having two-thirds of your body in front of the golf ball.

I've seen a lot of golfers playing the ball back in their stance while leaning the shaft and weight forward. When you do that at the setup, you will have to reverse your weight shift, falling back on your weight during your follow-through. This affects the bottom of your arc, and you will be inconsistent at best, struggling to get the ball out of the bunker. That's why I see a lot of golfers who set up this way struggle to get off their right foot during their finish.

3.   On the backswing, do not take the club too far to the inside. You want the club farther in front of you. Taking the club back inside is going to encourage hitting the sand too close to the golf ball or skulling the shot. Be sure that the club doesn't roll back on your backswing. This also puts the club more behind you. As soon as your arm moves toward your right hip pocket rather than traveling up toward your right shoulder, the golf club will get stuck behind. A stuck position is referred to as the right elbow low and under and behind the right chest and shoulder. Getting in this position will not allow the correct angle of attack for a good bunker shot.

This can also happen when you use too much hand action during your backswing. This means that you are snatching the golf club with your hands only, and this will not allow your shoulders to rock more vertically on the backswing.

Being too level with your shoulder going back on a bunker shot is not an ideal way to create the proper angle of attack.

4. Avoid too much hip rotation on the backswing during a bunker shot. That gets the club stuck behind you. Try to maintain the same hip position as you have on your setup. So on the top of your backswing, be sure that your right hip does not rotate. Maintain the same flex on the right leg as you set it at the address position. Hold that position as you go backward. It will almost feel as though you're squatting into your right hip on the backswing. Do not let your lower body rotate by allowing your hips to go backward on the backswing. This will help you to ensure that you keep the club from getting too far to the inside by taking it too low to the ground on the backswing.

# FAIRWAY BUNKER 16

## Choke Up, Dig In, Pick It

The long greenside bunker shots and fairway bunker shots can be the toughest shots in golf. This is because there are many decisions that must be made to execute them. Some golfers choose to blast them out of the sand with a sand wedge using a full swing, or take an extra club with a pitching wedge, or even take a 9 iron and blast the ball out by hitting the sand first, as in a normal greenside bunker shot.

There are many different types of fairway bunker shots. One of the best fairway bunker shots that I have ever seen live is the shot that Tiger Woods struck on the 18th hole at the Canadian Open in 2001. When that shot was struck, Tiger had a bunker lip that he had to clear with a long shot over 200 yards. He took a 6 iron and hit it out of the bunker as crisply as I've seen anyone ever hit one. It was one of his best fairway bunker shots. He picked the ball without even hitting the sand, or at least it looked that way. It was hit so level and picked so cleanly.

One of the keys to getting out of the fairway bunker successfully is first to evaluate the shot that you are facing and decide which club will clear the lip of the bunker. Once that decision is made, the second question you should consider is whether you should try to reach the green or, rather, plan for your next shot. Playing to your next shot, you must position the ball to the strength of your game. If the strength of your game is playing from 100 yards, then that's where you should lay up to. Hitting out of the fairway bunker without the option to reach the green, and playing the shot without the next shot in mind, would be a mistake. You are randomly taking a chance, as opposed to strategizing and planning and managing your game. With that being said, if you can reach the green after considering the lie and the stance, then go for it.

The process is to go through your pre-shot routine to best select which option you are trying to achieve. Every fairway bunker shot will be different. It is important to make the right decision before you take a club out of your bag. Sometimes the best shot is to play it safe and put the ball back into play for the next shot. The pros train themselves to go through this process. I have seen many players add strokes, causing them to lose championships when they do not select the right club. When you are facing challenges with a lie or hindered with a big lip of a bunker, the risk and reward may not be available. If you are not playing well and are hitting the ball poorly, your best shot is to play it safe by placing the ball back in the fairway.

Sometimes hitting sideways across the fairway to clear a bunker and put the ball back in position for your next shot is the best play. Hit the shot that's necessary, and do not play the heroic shot when it does not call for it. The last thing you want to face is to repeat the same shot in the bunker and to be forced on the next shot into playing it safe back in the fairway after you have made a mistake. Keep in mind that the bunker is a hazard, and you must play it as a hazard.

Now let's discuss the best technique to use and ways to play out of the fairway bunkers. We have discussed the pre-shot routine. Once that has been established and you have selected the shot to play, it is now time to know how to execute the shot.

Before I discuss how to play the fairway bunker shot step by step, let's first discover the feel and the visual imagery that has helped many players. The visual you want to have when hitting the fairway bunker is to imagine that the ball is sitting on a cart path. When the ball is on a cart path, the last thing you would want to do is to hit down on the ball, crashing the club into the concrete. Instead, you want to try to pick the ball and not scuff the bottom of the club.

That is the same feeling that you want to have when hitting a fairway bunker shot. You don't want to crash into the sand, causing the club to dig down deep into the sand. Hitting down sharply does not work consistently. You must pick or sweep the golf ball, which helps you to catch the ball clean.

Keeping this image in mind will help you to master the technique that I will be discussing in the next step. What you are trying to eliminate is a sharp angle of attack where the club is going down steep into the sand. What you are trying to achieve is a level, flatter impact area.

This is also not a bad idea to have when you are trying to hit a fairway wood or a long- to mid-iron off the fairway. When playing off the fairway with a long club, the last thing you want to take is a deep divot that will also put too much spin on the ball. You will lose distance by having the ball climb up rather than piercing the air on a driving flight.

The only time when you will want to head down sharply is with a shorter pitching wedge or lofted club to control spin and distance. Putting spin on a wedge is good, especially when you are hitting to tucked pin placements on the green. It is also good when you are around a greenside bunker and have the club open and are using the bounce of the club. There are specialty shots that demand a sharp angle of attack. The wedge should not be used for long distances. You need to sweep the club when you are using long irons or fairway woods in the fairway bunker.

The correct technique for this shot is to play the ball in the middle or toward the front of your stance. Then take a stance that's wider than normal. The wider stance will help you to encourage a flatter hitting area at impact. (Remember, a narrow stance and leaning forward is encouraged on short pitch shots, thus encouraging a downward strike with added backspin.) Then, build a firm base with your feet by digging at least one-half to one inch into the sand. Next, grip the club properly by choking down at least a half inch to one inch. It is a good idea to take an extra club or even two to allow for the difference of choking down on the club.

Keep in mind that the farther back you place the golf ball in your stance, the steeper the club is going to be at contact. Most golfers do this because they want to be sure to hit the ball first. Unfortunately, it works the opposite way. The more you have the ball forward in your stance, the more you will catch the ball cleanly.

While swinging the club, you will need to keep your feet quiet. The left foot should not come off the ground. This will have you swinging three-quarters of the full swing. Only the upper body swings. This helps you to swing in control and will prevent you from slipping. It will also prevent you from falling off balance. These are good techniques to attain success in the fairway bunker.

You can become an excellent fairway bunker player by practicing and implementing these techniques on the practice range. Practice different lies, such as downhill, uphill, and the ball above and below your feet. When you practice these shots, remember to swing with the slope. If you go with the slope, there will be a smooth follow-through. When you are going against the slope, you will feel resistance from the sand. Avoid that "stuck" feeling during your swing.

# THE HARDEST SHOT IN GOLF

CHAPTER
17

The long greenside bunker shot is referred to as the toughest shot in golf. This is because most golfers do not hit this shot with the proper technique. Instead, they hit the shot as if it were a regular greenside bunker shot. They swing harder to increase their distance. The problem with this is your margin of error. If you hit the ball first, using a full swing, you will send the ball across the green and out of play. Another way I see golfers hitting these shots is to play them with a pitching wedge or 9 iron, keeping the clubface slightly open. The problem with this is that if you use any other club but a sand wedge, there will be no bounce on the bottom of the club. Therefore, you are using the leading edge, and it will dig into the sand. The error in this scenario is that you are now bringing the leading edge into a bunker shot rather than sliding the club under the ball. You are now digging with the leading edge of the club, and it will go too deep into the sand. But if you know what to do and how to hit the shot with the proper technique, you will be able to control distance and spin every single time.

So, how do you hit this shot with the proper technique? First, you must approach the long greenside bunker shot as if it were a regular pitch shot. If it's a 40-yard long bunker shot around the green, you must hit this shot as if it were a 40-yard pitch shot from the fairway. The only difference is that instead of keeping your weight favored on the left side, you would set up having your weight equally distributed and picking the ball off the sand.

It is important to remember that you are no longer in a digging mode with the club in the sand; rather, you are swinging, leveling with the surface on the downswing. You are now trying

to pick the ball. To play this shot, the ball should be in a normal position or slightly forward as if you were hitting a regular fairway shot. This will create a shallow swing. Any time you lean forward favoring the weight on your front foot, as if you were hitting a normal pitch or a normal greenside bunker shot where the weight is 60 to 70 percent on the left side, you're creating a steep angle of attack. Swinging normally with an evenly distributed setup allows you to have a much flatter impact area to catch the ball clean.

There may be occasions when you encounter uneven lies, such as a downhill lie, uphill lie, ball above your feet, or ball below your feet. In these situations, make sure you lean with the slope. When you do this, your chance of getting out of the long greenside bunker with success will greatly increase. With practice, you will no longer view this as the toughest shot in golf.

# HIGH AND LOW SWINGS

## 18

During the 1997 Doral Open, I spent the day with Justin Leonard, one of the rising stars at that time on the PGA Tour. He is best known for his long and improbable putt that went in the hole during a match with José María Olazábal at the Ryder Cup in 1999 at Brookline Golf Club in Brookline, Massachusetts.

He is an exceptional ball striker, and he plays by feel. This type of player by definition is someone who doesn't think much about the mechanics of the swing but who is more artistic in his approach to hitting different golf shots. Justin's teacher asked him to hit different shots on command. I watched him hit the fade, draw, straight, low, and high shots. He would feel every shot toward the target. Every shot he hit was flawless.

One of the interesting things was that as he prepared to hit the different shots, he changed his body position to produce them. But, he only used one swing to hit all of them. The ball position varied for all the shots he hit. The high shots were in the front of his stance, and the low shots were in the back of his stance. Even though the swing was the same, the dynamics during his swings changed. Whether you're a feel player or a mechanical player, you must always apply the basics to hit the shots. Here are the basics and the mechanics to pull off these shots to control trajectory.

To hit the ball high, when you are addressing the ball, hold the club up at the top end more than you usually would. The longer you can hold the club, the easier it will be for the club shaft to kick the ball up in the air. Position the ball toward the front of your stance. The ideal position is inside the left heel, in a similar position as you would play your driver.

As you look down at the club, the shaft will lean backward, sitting behind your hands and head, which will be behind the ball at address. The clubface will be facing skyward. You will have up to 80 percent of your weight on your back foot for this shot. During your follow-through, you will hang back more than usual, with your body and your head behind the ball. This helps to add loft on your club, thus allowing the ball to start higher than normal and climb up farther. On the finish, the weight is on your back foot, with your hands and arms higher than usual.

It is important to note that the harder you swing, the higher the ball will go. The speed of the club and how hard you swing at the ball will have a tremendous amount of influence on how high it will travel. If you are looking for more distance, it is more advantageous to take a lesser club such as 5 iron and turn it into an effective 6 iron, using this technique to get both height and distance.

In most cases, when you want to hit the ball high, you are trying to clear a tree or an obstacle that stands in front of your ball. The key thing to remember is that the ball will not travel as far, because more of the ball's energy is being used to lift it up in the air. So, taking an additional club to get the full distance you are trying to achieve while getting the height necessary to clear your obstacle is something that you need to consider before hitting the ball.

When you are trying to hit the ball low, reverse everything you did to hit the ball high. When you are addressing the ball, hold the club farther down the shaft. The more you can choke down on the club, holding it shorter, the stiffer it will make the club, making it easier for the club to keep the ball down low.

When hitting the ball low, position the ball toward the back of your stance. The ideal position is on the inside of the right heel. The shaft will lean forward, setting it in the front of your hands. Also, your head is in front of the ball position at address. The clubface will be facing downward toward the ground. The face of the club should look flat from the top of the club to the leading edge. You will have up to 80 percent of your weight on your front foot. During your follow-through, you will be ahead of the ball more than usual, with your body and your head in front of the ball. You will start this way, and you will need to increase that position as you work through the ball.

This helps to de-loft the club, thus allowing the ball to start lower than normal and stay down. On the finish, the weight is on your front foot, with your hands and arms lower than normal. The more softly you swing, the lower the ball will travel. The speed of the club and how easily you swing at the ball will have a tremendous effect on how low it will travel. After practicing this, you will learn to control the height of the ball and play in any condition.

This is important on specialty shots, where you have to either clear a tree or stay below a branch line. The other advantage of controlling the height of the ball comes into play in windy conditions. Learning to control your trajectory will help you to play better when it's windy and allow you to escape trouble areas.

# FOCUS ON LOOSE ARMS CHAPTER 19

Keeping your arms loose and fluid during your golf swing is a must. There are three checkpoints that you have to consider to make sure that you are swinging properly.

First, at the address position, you must relax the arms so that you have a tension-free swing. When you are addressing the golf ball, you should have movements in your feet to allow the arms to waggle back and forth. It is important to feel the arms keeping constant tension in the hands. Before taking the club away, one of the last thoughts that you should consider is keeping your arms soft at the takeaway. This helps you to allow the proper load in the club and the proper sequence in which the club will set at the right place at the right time as the body rotates to the top of your swing.

Second, at the top of the swing, you must feel that the arms are in a soft position. Having a soft arm position at the top of your swing will allow your body to have the correct downswing transition.

The correct sequence from the top of your swing is to allow your body to shift your weight into the downswing. The soft arms will allow you to have a slight pause at the top prior to the downswing. The arms cannot have tension at the top of your swing, because if they do, they will begin the downswing ahead of the body, and not the other way around. This is not what you want. When this happens, it will affect the path of the club, causing either an unwanted early release or an over-the-top move in your downswing. This will cause either a slice or a pull shot and randomness in making ball contact.

The tension does increase during the backswing, but because it happens in less than a second, you do not feel where it gets tight. The top of your swing is your only checkpoint to feel how soft your arms should be before moving into the downswing. When you keep your arms soft, your body is moving on the downswing before your arms reach the top of your swing. This is the correct sequence that allows the body to lead the swing. With too much tension in the arms, it will affect the correct sequence that you must have from this position.

Third, at the finish position of your swing, your arms should feel soft. Relaxed and soft arms allow you to maintain a nice balanced position at your finish. This ensures that your arms are swinging freely toward your target. When you feel tension in your arms, you are pulling your arms in toward your body and shortening the extension in your arms. This affects the length of the arc and pulls the club up above the ball, causing you to top the ball or catch the upper part of the ball.

I see many golfers trying to keep their arms straight while working on their swing extension. Unfortunately, that will have the reverse effect. Both arms have a short period where they are straight. The rest of the time, they need to be soft enough to allow them to fold before the impact position and at the post-impact position. On the follow-through, the right arm extends while the left arm folds. It is only at impact and just past impact that both arms are straight. The rest of the time, the arms need to fold around the body. The right arm folds on the backswing and left arm folds on the follow-through. Again, there is also tension in the follow-through, but the arms should not feel it during the time you're swinging, as this happens naturally.

If you were to gauge the tension level on the follow-through, it is held firm; on a scale of 1 to 10, it would be an 8. This is because you are making contact, and you must hold the club tightly. This is something that is more instinctive. Your goal is to stay as soft with the arms as possible and to use these three checkpoints during your swing. These are great tips to have when you are playing under pressure, so you can stay more relaxed and natural throughout your swing.

Today, golf has so much focus on keeping the left heel down on the backswing. It is important to understand the foot and heel movements, as well as their purpose, during the swing. Keeping the left heel down on the backswing can be a good thing when you use shorter clubs. It helps to control your swing.

When you are driving the ball and you want to maximize your distance, you must be moving your feet correctly. The freedom of your swing that comes from the left heel coming off the ground is absolutely crucial to avoid tension. Tension in some parts of the swing is important, but in the full swing, it will kill the swing.

If you are flexible and the left heel does not come off the ground naturally, you can keep it in that position. Golfers with less flexibility can lift the heel off the ground for a full turn on their backswing. Most long hitters lift their heel off the ground during their full swing. Jason Day, Tiger Woods, and Bubba Watson all lift their heels off of the ground when driving the ball.

The left heel comes off the ground to allow the left foot to balance on its toes. This allows the heel to plant on the downswing. This should be the first part of the downswing. This was Jack Nicklaus's signature move. Whether you believe in the modern golf swing or a classic swing, this move should be a part of your full swing. Bubba Watson claims that he never takes golf lessons and that he plays by feel. His front foot comes off the ground more than anyone on the PGA tour, making him one of the longest hitters.

To execute this position correctly, you will first need to swing back to the top of your backswing. At this point, the club is parallel to the ground. Be sure to allow your left heel to come off the ground and to balance on your toes. You will notice that this movement allows the backswing to get longer and fuller at the top. It is crucial in enabling the full circle of your swing.

One of the ways to practice this is without a golf club. Set up in an athletic golf position, turn your shoulders and hips fully, and balance on your left toes. This will give you a sense of how your body should move. Do this three or four times without the club, then do this with the club. This will help train your lower body.

When you learn this footwork, your swing will slow down and have better rhythm. Keeping your heel down on the ground encourages a quick tempo. This hinders your ball striking, because it makes it harder to hit the center of the clubface by throwing off the sequence of your swing.

Stamp your heel on the ground; this will allow you to shift your weight properly. At this point, your back is still facing the target as you are still fully turned. Place the heel on the ground while the upper body falls forward, allowing your left foot to catch the weight as it is going forward. The pressure you feel will be on your knees and on your upper thigh.

A good drill is to place your left hand on the right pocket of your pants; your body will not yet have reached the end of your backswing. With your left heel off the ground, your shoulders are fully turned. Then from there, while you keep your upper body coiled at the full turn, put your left heel down on the ground and allow the weight to transfer onto your left leg. The weight should transfer about 70 percent at this point.

Next, you are going to turn your body toward the ball. To turn, simply release the left hand holding the right hip pocket; that allows you to rotate. When you get the shift correct, it automatically engages the correct rotation as the next phase in your swing.

This is a simple way to learn how to work your feet. The heel is the first part of your transition on the downswing. Allowing the heel to lift off the ground is a good source of power.

# DIFFERENT PRESSURES FOR DIFFERENT SHAPES 20

When you're trying to curve the golf ball in different directions, you must maintain the grip pressure in a manner that encourages the shot. For instance, if you're hitting a fade or a slice, your grip should be held more tightly, especially in the last three fingers of your top hand, which allows the pulling motion. This helps to hold off the release of the golf club. Holding off the release in the swing means that you are now trying to prevent the clubface from releasing. This allows the left hand to stay on top of the right as you pull through impact.

During the follow-through, due to the tighter grip pressure on the left hand, your left shoulder will pull up and will finish higher on the follow-through as the elbows are pulling through. This will not allow the clubface to rotate. Therefore, the knuckles of your left hand will face up, just as your right hand palm will. This will guarantee a slice or fade swing. Typically, when someone is trying to fade the ball, this is similar to the feeling that he or she is trying to have in his or her swing. Holding the club more tightly will allow the body to outpace the hands when you finish your swing. Your body may be at a finish position, but the hands are lagging behind and will finish under the shoulders.

The reverse side of this is that if you're drawing the golf ball, you must hold the grip loosely or lightly on the club. This encourages the club to flip over the swing and to rotate the face of the club. This, in turn, allows the body to slow down on the swing. A lighter grip pressure speeds the hands up, activating them more during the follow-through. This allows the center of your body to remain still as you go through the ball. The right shoulder will finish higher because of the hands rotating over to the right side. This will encourage a hook or a draw.

Holding your hands more lightly encourages this motion of releasing the club properly. Grip pressure on a scale of 1 to 10 should be about a 2. You want to feel this grip pressure at the address position, at the top of the backswing, and at the follow-through. Remember, this is the three-checkpoint system. The grip pressure increases throughout the swing, but your goal is to try to hold it as soft as possible. This allows the rotation of the hands and arms to speed up the club throughout the release. Keep in mind that the grip pressure has a tremendous influence on the clubface. If you slice the ball, keep your grip looser, and if you hook the ball hold the grip tighter. These different grip pressures help you to control the direction of your shot correctly.

# DRAW SWING PREFERRED

## 21

In the case of the draw shot, the ball works right to left for the right-handed golfer, and it is the most preferred golf shot for all players. Professional golfers use this shot the most. It requires the most powerful swing, and it maximizes the inside path of the swing without coming over the top of the ball.

To play this shot, you must have the club coming from the right path, and the clubface must be pointing square to your target or just slightly closed. How much of your swing path is traveling from the inside and where the club points will determine how much of a draw you will hit. Regardless of how much the ball curves, as long as the clubface angle is not severely closed to the target, the shot will be a powerful one.

When we look at the history of professional golfers who are the most powerful hitters, they have always struggled with hitting too much of a draw, which turns the shot into a hook. The slice, however, is the weakest shot in golf. Unfortunately, this is how many amateur golfers hit their golf shot. In an effort to learn how to draw the golf ball, you must learn how to come down from the inside of the swing and then out toward the target and on to your finish.

On the backswing, you have three options to choose from when taking the club back. First, you can take it straight back onto your swing plane. Second, you can take it outside of your swing plane. Third, you can go on the inside of your swing plane. No matter which path a player chooses in taking the club back,

most professionals return the club to the inside of their swing or right on their swing plane. This is the desired path. With the clubface square to their target or slightly to the left, it produces a ball draw.

To get the path started correctly from the top of your swing, you must start the downswing transition properly. This means that your body first has to shift to allow the club to drop to the inside of your swing path. I discuss this position quite extensively in the downswing section of the book. So, as you transition to the inside of your swing, the key from this point is to allow the arms and hands to extend out away from your body, swinging toward your target, creating width on the follow-through. This is also referred to as the full extension in your follow-through. It allows the arms and hands to rotate and turn the club over, allowing the forearms to cross over. This is where most golfers feel the snap in their golf swing. The rotation of the forearms crossing over each other allows the club to reach its maximum clubhead speed.

It is important to square the club at the target and allow the face of the club to rotate over the ball, which allows the ball to curve right to left. Your hands and arms can generate a lot of speed in the golf swing, especially when you learn to rotate the club back and snap the club into an L position on the forward swing. Many of the top amateur golfers and professionals who played golf in the old days used their arms and hands very actively. This was because the clubs were very low-tech. Today, the clubs are made with steel shafts that yield a much stiffer flex in the club. Now you see most of the top amateurs and professional golfers using their body to leverage the club more and hitting the ball with greater force. So with the equipment changes, the body has synchronized the follow-through along with the release of the hands.

One of the drills that is very helpful in learning how to release the club properly is first to stand with your feet no more than three inches apart. Hover the club about a foot above the ground. Then, swing the club back and forth around your body, allowing the club to hinge on the backswing into an L position and hinging the club on the forward swing into an L position, as

well. This should create a mirror image of each other, back and through on both sides of the swing.

Do this drill until you can hear the swishing of the club at the bottom of the swing. The arms should remain soft. You should hold the club tension-free, and there should be no tension in your body movements.

To encourage a draw swing, the right arm needs to cross over to the left (see first image on page 187). This allows the club to release. Also, allow the clubface to rotate so that it is closing down on your follow-through.

There should be an effort to allow the clubhead to create power by releasing past your hands and to avoid a block position in your swing.

A block swing occurs when the top of the right hand after impact is underneath the left hand. The club will be dragging behind your hand.

This is the classic block position in the golf swing that will guarantee that the clubface will stay open, thus making the ball go right. Without the clubface rotation, you are guaranteed a slice.

This may happen if you grip the club too strongly. But if you have a good grip in a moderate position, this should not happen. It is only the rare golfer who has an extremely close or a strong grip and can pull this off and hit the ball straight. But to do the block-and-hold move, you would have to contort your body on the follow-through. This will eventually hurt your back due to so much tension put on it during the follow-through. It is not a recommended swing.

The right hand should feel like you are hitting a topspin forehand in tennis. This creates topspin on the ball, and it will do the same thing in golf. In a golf shot, it will allow the ball to climb up and out, turning over and spinning in a right-to-left direction. This is a powerful shot in golf. It involves coming from the inside of your swing, then swinging out toward your target in an inside-out path, and allowing the face of the club to rotate on the release.

Because golf courses nowadays are extremely long, distance matters, and playing courses from 6,800 yards to 7,000-plus yards long is normal for most great new courses. You must have power and control. Learning to curve the ball right to left gives you predictability and control of direction.

Keep in mind that you are not trying to overspin it too much, as that would be bad. If you do this, the ball will not stay up in the air long enough to maximize distance. But the proper release allows the clubhead and the face to rotate so that it avoids a slice or a push to the right. If you are someone who struggles to hit the ball to the right side of the golf course, this will help you to control and to correct your swing. A block or slice position is the weakest shot in golf.

Another drill you can do that will help you to hit the draw is to swing the club with your right hand only. The right hand is your release hand in the golf swing. The left hand supports as your guide hand. It's naturally designed to pull, which encourages a block move in your swing. But if you make the right forearm and hand turn over (imagine a topspin tennis stroke during your swing), this will create the proper release.

So that being said, hold the club with your right hand only, and turn the club up slightly, using your wrist. Hover the club approximately a foot above the ground. From there, swing back and forth, allowing the right hand to feel the rotation. Another way to visualize this is if you are doing the right-hand-only drill; after impact, rotate your right hand down so that the palm of your hand is facing the ground as you swing through.

A block position occurs when your right hand or palm is facing up toward the sky. When you do that, you will notice that the clubface will not rotate downward. The clubhead also will not release past your hands. It is essentially like a long putt. You are no longer swinging at but stroking the ball. You would only want to use the stroke in putting and in chipping, because it is good for short-distance control shots, not for creating power.

This will give you a sense of a release and of a block swing. Blocking the release enforces a slice or a block to the right. Knowing the difference between the two will help you to practice correctly.

As the arms swing back and forth, allow them to attach to your body on both sides. Arms and body need to work together in these movements. Do this, and you will feel a connection between your arms and your upper chest area. A slight tension to keep the top of your arms attached to your body will allow your arms to swing and your body to rotate as one piece.

Once you have made this connection between the arms and body, take your normal stance. The feet should be apart, thus creating a firm base to handle a harder swing. Now, let's apply this feel to the drills.

Take your normal stance, your arms attached again to your body, but now with your feet wider in an athletic setup. From there, move the swing back and forth with both of your heels coming off the ground. There should be movement in your toes. Your arms should be hanging on, back and through.

Allow your feet, knees, and hips to move together with your club along with your upper body. It's as if you were dancing with the club. After you learn how to move fluidly into these positions, you will learn to create leverage with your arms while taking a full swing. This will generate almost full speed in the golf club.

Once you have learned how to brush the ground with this swing, you are ready to start clipping the tee.

This was Harvey Penick's favorite drill. I love this drill because it allows you to learn a swing and make it more permanent before introducing a golf ball. This helps the process, because it eliminates the acquisition of bad habits.

Once you have learned to clip the tee and take it off the ground, you are ready to introduce the ball and start hitting it off the tee. Do not let this deter you from practicing off a tee in the beginning. This is the way professionals practice when they are learning a new swing or trying to groove a new swing. This only helps to make your swing better.

Practice with your 7 iron and work up to a 5 iron, but do this over and over again when you are learning to release the club and to make the ball go from right to left.

# TWO STEPS FOR THE
# DRAW AND THE FADE

There are many ways to curve the ball intentionally. The ball reacts to where the clubface is at impact. It can be open, square, or closed to your target. And it reacts to where your swing path is, which is directly at your target, to the right of your target, or to the left of your target. These are the only ways that a club can come in to hit the ball at impact.

The best way to curve the ball intentionally is to align your body to where you would like the ball to start. Then, aim the clubface in the direction where you would like the ball to curve and end up. If you are faced with a situation where you must curve the ball around a tree or any other obstacle on the golf course, this is one of the ways to bend the ball in either direction.

For example, if you want the ball to curve to the right, you should aim the club to the right. Depending on where you would like the ball to start in the direction for the curve, you should aim your body on that line. Next, place the club on the ground and aim the clubface to where you would like the ball to end up. Then, grip the club after you have established the clubface direction. This allows the body direction and the club direction to be opposite. Follow these steps to position yourself correctly to curve the ball intentionally. The incorrect way to do this would be to already have taken the grip first and then aimed your body to the left of your target and put the club down toward the target without changing your grip on the club. This will not change the direction of the club, since the club is square to your path.

Remember, the ball curves when the path of your swing and clubface angle conflict. When the paths of the swing and club-face angle are lined up in the same direction at impact, the ball will go straight. Knowing this ball flight rule is crucial to understanding why you misdirect the ball and to knowing the cure to the problem. Hitting an intentional hook or a draw shot would be the direct opposite of these positions. You will aim the club left of your body's alignment and grip the club.

This makes these shots predictable and consistent because you're not making any changes to your swing to get the curve. I remember during a high school match we played at Frenchmen's Creek Golf Club in Palm Beach, Florida. We were playing against Gary Nicklaus, who played for Benjamin Preparatory School. I got to watch Jack Nicklaus practice with his coach, Jack Grout. He was practicing different shots on the range. As he was working the ball in all directions, I noticed that his swing looked the same. He moved his body around the ball, making adjustments in his setup to hit the different shots. I was amazed at how he could do so many things with the ball.

For Jack, it was simple to work the ball in either direction, because he controlled the shots with the direction of his club. He didn't change his grip. He adjusted the club in his hands. He would turn the club, then grip it. It was so simple and incredibly effective. I remember going out to the driving range at Martin County Golf Course afterward and practicing these shots and copying everything that he did. It was so enlightening to me how I could easily control the direction of the ball without changing anything else in my golf swing.

Clearly, when you are hitting different shots, it's the simple things that matter the most. What I remember from his practice session was that he laid a couple of clubs on the ground. He put one on the target line, and the other one he used as a guide for his setup. His shoulders, hips, feet, and even his eyes would line up square to the shaft on the ground. I can't tell you how important it was for me to watch how the best player in the previous century practiced. With his teacher, Mr. Grout, he would practice the fundamentals over and over again and day after day. This showed me how important the fundamentals of golf were to Jack Nicklaus. He honed his swing year after year but never made major changes to it. The basic fundamentals are the foundation of your game. A lot of amateurs fail to recognize this. You should never underestimate the importance of the grip, club alignment, and setup and balance points, and how they affect each golf shot and ball position.

The biggest reason for your swing to change unintentionally over time is that you are not paying attention to the ball position and you begin to play too far forward or too far back in your stance. Then your swing will start to chase that ball that is not in the right setup position. The swing will either come over the top or your body will lunge at the ball. If the swing is too far forward in your stance or is hanging back, you will start to play the ball too far back in your stance.

If you're trying to work the ball left to right or to fade the ball away from the tree, you would first do the same thing by aiming your body left of that tree in front of you, and be sure to give yourself enough space to avoid hitting the tree. Then from there, point the club in a direction where you'd want to ball to land. And one of things to keep in mind is that with the club that you're using on the fade, the ball will not go as far. For instance, if you're hitting a 5 iron and you are slicing or fading the ball to the right, what will happen is that you are effectively turning the 5 iron into a 7 iron.  If you are bold, go at least one to two clubs up, depending on how much you're trying to curve the ball; so, on a fade or a slice, add an extra club or two to allow for this to take place. This is also true for a draw or a hook. If you're intentionally hooking the ball, you will de-loft the club at impact. This means that the dynamics that impact you will be decreasing the loft in the club, so the ball will go lower. Something to keep in mind when you are working in both directions on a fade or a slice: the ball will not curve as much if you are trying to hit a lofted club.  If you are expecting a ball to curve, or slice, left-to-right, you will not get the right result with a lofted club such as your 9 iron or pitching wedge. It's the same thing if you're trying to draw or hook the ball with a low-lofted club such as a 3 iron or 4 iron, because the ball will not stay up in the air high enough to allow the curve to take its course, and dynamically, it is harder to hook a lower number club then it is to take a higher number club and de-loft it, allowing the ball to curve. Understanding the dynamics of how the club is designed and what it's designed to do is important when you are selecting the right club for the intentional movement of the ball.

Also remember, hooking the golf ball will generally roll it out much farther after it hits the ground because of the topspin that you are creating. Generally, when the ball is hitting the ground with a draw or hook, it is coming in lower, and like a topspin forehand in tennis, the ball will be moving much faster once it lands. A fade or a slice is the opposite; when the ball hits the ground it will drop softly and will not roll out. Knowing the difference between these two shots and how they will react once they hit the ground will help you to know how to approach your shot for total distance. You will need to carry the ball more with a slice to get the total distance, and with a draw you will need to plan to hit shorter to the desired target and allow it to roll out the rest of the way to the hole.

Having the understanding of how to curve the golf ball and what clubs would be the best choice to curve it in one direction or the other is very important. This understanding helps in controlling direction. Then, it's important to understand how the ball would react once it hits the ground—either it will roll out or it will stop. Knowing those two situations will help you to play this particular golf shot better. With practice, you will master the shot much more quickly than you would expect. Then you can execute this shot with ease.

# ROUGH IT 23

Hitting a golf ball out of the rough can be a challenge for most golfers, because they don't know how the ball will react. One thing you can be sure of is that if there is high grass behind your ball, the heel of the club will snag and close down the clubface, depending on which club you're hitting. The ball will either go left or hard left after it leaves the clubface, depending on the speed with which you swing the club.

In order to play this shot successfully, you must do two things. Let's use a clock as an example to show where the proper position of the golf club is at address for the high rough shots. If you are looking at the leading edge of the club when it is straight up and down, the top of the club is at 12 o'clock and the bottom is at 6 o'clock. The first thing you must do when you grip the golf club is open the clubface to the 1 o'clock position. If you are in very thick rough, then you should probably turn the clubface to the right to the 2 o'clock position. Then grip the golf club as you would normally do, so that you are now addressing the ball out of the rough with the clubface open.

The other thing to remember in this swing is during the backswing, cock the club up more with your wrist than you do with your normal swing. The sharp angle of attack during your swing will help the ball cut through the grass better. This is important, because the club needs to dig a little bit more into the rough so that the ball can come out more easily. Due to the height and the thickness of the grass, the clubface will close at impact. During the swing, you must grip the club more tightly during contact and at the follow-through.

Tight grip pressure is very important as you drive that club through the rough. You'll notice that the follow-through is very limited through the rough. This is what you want to feel and expect during this shot. It will not feel the same on the follow-through as a normal swing from the fairway. It will also be more abbreviated, and the follow-through will stop at your shoulder level or slightly below it. Remember to take a wider stance than normal so you can create the leverage necessary during this swing. The wide stance will help you, because you will swing harder in order to get the ball out of the heavy rough.

Sometimes I see amateurs trying to hit long irons and even woods out of the high rough. They find themselves with the ball not moving very far due to the thickness of the rough and the loft the ball needs to jump off out of the high grass. When you are in the high, thick grass, the best choice is to get the ball back in play in the fairway. It is necessary to choose a higher-lofted club. This will make cutting through the high grass a lot easier than if you're using a club with very little loft. The shorter the golf club you use with a high loft, the more vertical the angle in your swing, which allows the golf club to have a sharper angle attack for this special shot. Do not try to hit a shot 200 yards or more out of a thick rough with a long iron or fairway club. Even the strongest of swings on the PGA Tour will have their challenges trying to get the ball up in the air and reach the green from this distance. The key thing is to take your medicine and put the ball back in play and place it in the best position for your next shot. The higher-lofted club will allow you to achieve this.

# FOCUS ON THE TOP HAND FOR CLUBFACE CONTROL CHAPTER 24

There are a lot of things that can influence the clubface angle throughout the swing. The left-hand grip has the most influence on the clubface angle.

If you're slicing the golf ball, the first thing you may want to check is to see where your top hand is positioned. One thing to help you to offset the slice that is going to the right is to turn the top hand to the right; it will help you to close the clubface to the left so that the ball doesn't slice. This puts your left grip in a stronger position. By turning your grip more to the right, it will instantly correct your clubface without doing anything else different to your swing. Too many golfers struggle with overthinking their golf swing when trying to fix a slice. This can become very frustrating and can make their swing worse.

If you are hooking the golf ball, turn your left hand more to the left. This puts the club in a weaker position. This will help you to offset the hook that is going to the left by opening the clubface more at impact. This will instantaneously fix your hook without making any other swing changes. In fact, this is the best way to fix the clubface angle for the direction. Adjusting the grip to hit the ball straighter is a fundamental process. It is also a great way to make the change in your ball flight immediately when you are out on the golf course and fighting a slice or hook.

Learning to do this will give you a great sense of clubface control. All great players have this in common. They know where the clubface positions are at all times. They feel the clubface when it is open, closed, or square at impact. Learning to adjust your grip will enable you to get a great sense of where the clubface is at all times, especially at impact.

# Section VII

## Putting It All Together

# WHY "FOCUS DRILLS"?

Now that you have learned the fundamentals, dynamics, and techniques of the game, you have to put it all together. The focus drills will help you to isolate and identify every aspect of your game that is important to improving your game.

The focus drills help you to build your golf swing and to make corrections to your swing. They cover everything from your grip to your putting and help you to identify the important aspects of every part of the game in order to improve your game more quickly. It is an accelerated way of learning to adapt to changes and to go through the process so that the changes you make are permanent. Without a focus, it is unclear from swing to swing what you're trying to achieve. The feeling of the golf swing changes throughout every shot. You need to pay attention to the task at hand, one swing at a time. Let's review some of the important focus drills in different areas of the game, from the fundamentals to the short game.

The "focus on the grip" drill is the "wringing of the towel" drill. You put the hands together so that they work together in a comfortable and natural way. No matter what type of grip you choose—the Vardon/overlapping, Interlock, or Ten-finger grip—this focus drill will get your grip in the right place. There are pressure points and grip pressures with which you hold the club to allow them to work together. Therefore, different shots demand different grip pressures. A light grip pressure is used for a draw swing that allows the hands to release the club at impact. A tight grip pressure, which helps you to keep the club-face from closing, helps you to hit fades and will also slice the ball away from your target.

The "focus on the address" drill targets the balance at your setup. You play golf on the insides of your feet. With both knees bent, you should feel the pressure on the insides of your knees, which are pinched slightly inward. You can feel this more in your right knee. You should feel your weight evenly over both feet. Feeling the weight evenly on most approach shots helps you to maintain your balance at address so that you can hit solid golf shots.

The "focus on the backswing" drill begins with a forward press that allows you to initiate the backswing with a forward motion that helps you to put the club in a natural position. There are two major "focus on the backswing" drills that allow you to be athletic and powerful during your coil. First is the initial part of the backswing that allows you to stay connected with the golf club. This lets the body and the club to work together in one single motion. In this position, the center of your body stays connected with the butt end of the golf club as it goes through the first stage of your backswing. This is about three feet away from the ball.

The other focus position is the last part, or top, of the backswing. You need to feel the full coil position on the inside of your right leg. This is like a pitcher on a mound who holds that weight on the inside of the right leg so that he is able to push off in a forward motion to throw the ball. Getting those two positions correct assures that you have made a powerful and athletic backswing.

The "focus on impact" drill allows you to understand where you are at the point of contact. This is one of the most important positions that allow the golf ball to hit the center of the golf club each and every time. Knowing this position forces you to focus on getting into a dynamic impact position. You will need to be on the left side at impact, with the hands leading the clubface at all times. The shaft should be leaning forward as it approaches every golf shot to create power. The flat left wrist position— where the wrist, the arm, and the shaft are all in one line—is one of the most important components of impact when you are playing good golf. This is one of the most common denominators that every great player's golf swing has. The amateurs come into this position with a cupped left wrist at impact, which is a very common move for someone who is hitting the ball randomly and not making consistent contact at impact. Once you master these impact positions, you will understand how to control the direction of the ball.

Understanding where the clubface is during impact is one of the most important parts of being consistent at ball striking. When the club position is square at impact, the ball will go straight. If the clubface is open at impact, the ball will go to the right. If the club is closed at impact, the ball will go left. Simply put, this is what makes the ball go in the direction in which you are hitting it. Understanding the "focus on impact" positions will help you to cure many misdirected golf shots.

The "focus on the downswing" drill will get you into the proper hitting position every time. When you do this correctly, you will master this position that all great golfers have in their golf swing. "Shift, rotate, and hit" is one of the most important things for you to remember at the top of your golf swing. This helps you make the correct transition and create powerful and consistent contact every single time. Until you can master this motion on your downswing, working on other parts of your swing such as the direction of the ball is less important. Remember, direction is not important until you can hit the ball solidly. This part of the swing helps you to master hitting the ball in the sweet spot.

In the "focus on the follow-through" drill, the club, body, and arms stay connected in front of you as you work past the ball. The swing is passing through impact almost three feet away from that position. The club needs to release fully where the butt end of the club is pointing at your sternum. This is as important as any other part of the swing, as it controls the flow of your swing after contact. Without it, you can take all that is good during your swing and still hit poor shots.

The "focus on driving the ball off the tee" drill allows the club to hover above the ground and swing in the air without taking a divot. The driver swing has different dynamics than the iron swing. So you must understand the fundamentals and differences in the setup to ensure that you are driving the ball correctly. In this case you are swinging the club at full speed. Allowing your swing to have full motion without restriction is one of the key elements to driving the ball well. Driving the ball doesn't necessarily mean hitting the ball as far as possible when playing a round of golf. It is more about placing the drive in the fairway to make your next shot.

The "focus on the short game" drill allows you to lower your score and to recover from errant approach shots. This aspect of the game becomes more important as you're working toward keeping a handicap or playing in a match to help you maximize your score. This part of the game is more than 50 percent of your total score. When you are trying to lower your score, this is the most important part of your game. Understanding Section V: Mastering the Short Game will help you to manage the technique and the system of lowering your score.

# PLAY TO YOUR STRENGTHS AND AVOID YOUR WEAKNESSES

## CHAPTER 26

Now that you've worked on your game and have improved on a lot of the techniques that we have discussed, you're ready to take your game out on the golf course.

To play the game well, you must learn to understand your game. Identifying the strengths and weaknesses in your game helps you to avoid many mistakes. If your weakness is hitting accurately off the tee with a driver, you may want to hit this shot with your 3 wood, which may be more a more effective club for you to use in order to put the ball in the fairway. The dynamics of a 3 wood give it additional loft. The angle makes the ball go up in the air, as opposed to a driver, which is a straighter-faced club that makes the ball spin sideways. The loft on the 3 wood allows you to spin the ball backward, which helps you to keep the ball straighter. So it is not necessarily taking the driver, but taking the right club, that will achieve your goal of hitting more fairways.

The other part of playing to your strengths and avoiding your weaknesses is your yardages. If, for instance, you are not comfortable hitting a shot from 100 yards and you feel more comfortable hitting from 130 or 150 yards, that is where you want to leave the golf ball for your approach shot. Have a strategy so that you can leave your ball in a place where you are comfortable playing from.

A pre-shot routine is an essential part of your game. The two aspects of a good pre-shot routine are the physical part and the mental part. The mental part of the pre-shot routine is getting behind the ball and evaluating what club and what shot you must play. The last thing you want to do is to just pull out a club for distance. Instead, you need to check for wind direction, uphill lies, downhill lies, and other factors that may affect the shot. Evaluate at the completion of your follow-through as you bring the club down in front of you. This is where you want to analyze your shot so that you can make the necessary corrections on your next swing. When you evaluate your shot, you need to decide what club and what type of swing you will need to use to make the shot.

For the physical part of your pre-shot routine, you will need to organize your grip and determine the line of your target and then set up to the ball. As you are walking into your setup, begin by picking an intermediate target in front of the golf ball to align yourself with your target. Walking toward the golf ball from the side will help you to be open to your target and see your shot much better. Set up to the ball with your right foot first, then square up to your target. From there, look at your target once and then look at the ball and repeat that at least twice. Make your best swing through the golf ball and into the finish. When you go through this routine, it will help you to take your game to the next level. Every top player has a pre-shot routine that they go through every single time before they hit a golf shot.

# ACHIEVING YOUR GOLFING GOALS CHAPTER 27

Set goals for yourself. Whether you are an aspiring touring professional, an aspiring amateur golfer, or you would just like to play respectably with your friends, be sure to go out and set expectations for yourself. You do that by understanding what it takes to achieve your golfing goals and putting in the time necessary to meet them. Golf is one of the most wonderful games in that, as in life, whatever you put into it is what you will get out of it.

The more you practice, the luckier you will get on the golf course with your shots. The game is not about hitting a perfect shot every single time. The better you get in your golf swing, the less your misses will get you in trouble. Trying to achieve perfection is the wrong thing to do in this game, because it will drive you crazy. This game is not a game of perfect.

If you hit the ball a short distance, look for game improvement clubs to help you to hit it farther and higher. Take advantage of the technology available to you. If you want to be more athletic, you can go to the gym and get more physically fit. All of these things will help you to improve and enjoy your golf game. No matter what your goals are, set an obtainable goal so that you are enjoying the process of improving your golf game!

# THE SCORING GAME

## 28

Approximately 50 percent of your score comes from playing from a hundred yards out to the hole. This is what we call the scoring part of the game, where you play mostly with your pitching wedge, sand wedge, and putter. This part of the game requires you to understand how to play with technique and by feel.

To learn how to improve your short game, you should start managing your distance from the short areas. You can practice by yourself with one or multiple balls before a round of golf. Throw the ball in a random area inside of a hundred yards. Hit the shot that is required for the situation, then walk up and try to see if you can make the putt to get up and down.

Figure out which part of the game—if it's your short approach or your putting—that is holding you back from getting the ball up and down. Find out which part of your game is weak, and typically you will find that your pitching or your chipping is not getting the ball close enough to the hole for you to make the putt. You can be a good putter and not hit the ball close enough with your wedge, which increases the odds that you will miss the putt. When someone comes to me for a lesson because they are struggling with their short game, and they say that they are not getting the ball up and down, one thing I notice is that they are not bad putters, but they are not chipping well. If you are hitting a putt outside of 10 feet, your chances of making the putt become less than 30 percent for most golfers. Improve your chipping the ball closer to the hole, and you will find that you will lower your score quickly.

# PRACTICE WITH A PURPOSE

CHAPTER

# 29

Practice makes permanent, so when you're practicing, practice perfect. Break your practice session down into the different segments of your swing. Practice smart by building a workstation around your swing so that it helps you to monitor what you're trying to master. Put a club down your target line and learn to set up square each and every time. Do this perfectly, because it is hard enough to go on the golf course and find your target and set up correctly. Understand what the correct alignment feels like during your practice session. Next, practice your backswing, downswing, and impact, and break all of these segments down so you can make changes more quickly. Doing these drills will isolate the specific parts of your swing so that you can make permanent changes.

When you are making changes, start practicing off a tee to create a perfect lie. This helps you to focus on the swing changes rather than trying to hit the ball perfectly off the ground. Don't be too proud to practice off a tee. When the pros are working to make swing changes, they practice off a tee. It is a more effective way to improve your swing. When making swing changes, select one movement at a time, and don't have any more than one thought at a time. This will help you to isolate a specific change and focus on a drill to accelerate your process.

Be sure you get organized before you swing. Remember to practice being brilliant at the basics. Understand that when you get these fundamentals correct, and rehearse your movements three times before striking a golf ball. Do not hit balls one after another. This only makes your swing worse by making whatever you are doing more permanent. Look where your divots are landing on the ground with a "focus on the line" drill, which is a line that represents where the ball is in between your feet. Be sure the divot is landing in front on the target side of the line. This means that you are hitting the ball first, which is important in making consistent contact with the ball. When you complete your swing, hold your finish and evaluate your shot. Ask yourself what the swing felt like and how the ball flew. Did it go as planned, or did it not? Ask why the ball moved left or right or why you missed the ball thin or caught the ground before the ball. Why did I miss the center of the clubface? These are the questions that you can find answers to when you practice, which will help you make progress in your game. Be sure to practice with a game plan in mind. Take notes about your game and your practices. Having something on paper is a great way to go back and remember the good thoughts and feelings that made your practice fun. Describe what you did not like about a certain day when you had a poor practice. Writing all of these things down can help you to improve more quickly and more effectively. All of this will help you to achieve your goals and get the most out of your game. Remember, always practice with a purpose!

ST. JOSEPH COUNTY
PUBLIC LIBRARY

OCT 1 8 2024

SOUTH BEND, IN